CULTURAL MIGRATION

A Short History of
Nkrankwanta and Anyii Dwabene

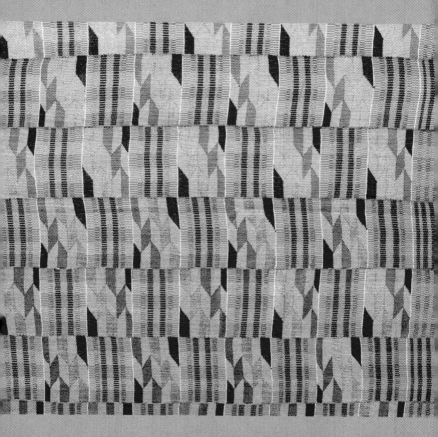

ZAC ADAMA

The cover design of *Cultural Migration: A Short History of Nkrankwanta and Anyii Dwabene* is a Kente motif. Kente is a popular traditional cloth made from cotton and woven on a hand loom. Kente comes from Ghana and Cote d'Ivoire. In design and output, Kente is an ensemble of a few colorful patterns woven into strips that are stitched together.

Weavers or sellers of Kente give their product a name. Typically, the name is a proverb, a statement of fact, or a popular say-say. Our book cover Kente motif has a Twi proverb for name:

"Kyɛmferɛ se ɔdaa hɔ akyɛ, na onipa a, ɔnwenee no nso nyɛ dɛn?"

Translated, "If the potsherd (a pottery fragment usually unearthed as an archaeological relic) is being boastful about longevity, what should the potter that moulded it in the first place, say?"

In interpretation, the Kente cover design of *Cultural Migration: A Short History of Nkrankwanta and Anyii Dwabene* reminds of the importance of time honored knowledge and experience as we explore our respective roots and heritage.

CULTURAL MIGRATION

A Short History of Nkrankwanta and Anyii Dwabene

Zac Adama

CULTURAL MIGRATION
A Short History of Nkrankwanta and Anyii Dwabene

iUniverse books may be ordered through booksellers or by contacting:

iUniverse
1663 Liberty Drive
Bloomington, IN 47403
www.iuniverse.com
1-800-Authors (1-800-288-4677)

ISBN: 978-1-4917-9467-8 (sc)
ISBN: 978-1-4917-9468-5 (e)

Library of Congress Control Number: 2016907042

Print information available on the last page.

iUniverse rev. date: 05/10/2016

For my girls: Amina and Bintu

But above all, for my late grandmother, whose undying love and encouragement prepared me for this task. To your memory, Moni Afua Seala, I dedicate this piece.

An Ode to She

She was never called Nana,
Five generations down,
Even as the less deserving
Got called Grandma.
A mark of endearment and adoration;
Love overflowing, in abundance.
Long-suffering without bitterness,
She that was a fountain of bottomless,
Patented generosity, wisdom, and patience.
A living example of what
Life herself ought to emulate.

The unknown wayfarer found a home in your home.
You, mother to orphans, giver of solace.
The destitute, downhearted, you encouraged.
Even the dreaded, distanced, and discarded—
You took them in and transformed.
You enriched the lives of so many.
Nearly all have drunk from your brimming cup
Of therapeutic succor, warmth, and humanity.

The many brought to be raised
Under your tutelage and motherly care,
To be trained in good manners and comport,
Values that enrich self and society.
You've educated the very educated,
Counseled seasoned counselors.
Mother Earth must be a proud parent,
To have produced a parent worthy to so many.
To you this song of praise,
Moni Afua Seala, a.k.a. Hajia Masara.

CONTENTS

PREFACE

This book is pioneering; it is intended to fill a vacuum. It is the first written account of the history of Ngala Ngwandaa (Nkrankwanta), a commercial and farming town in the Brong Ahafo Region of Ghana. Nkrankwanta lies on the geographical coordinates of N 7°1'9" W 3°2'35".

Cultural Migration: A Short History of Nkrankwanta and Anyii Dwabene is also a subject in social anthropology. It explores and navigates some of the cultural basics and the worldview of the Anyii people. The Anyii are a member of the larger Akan ethnic group that dominates both Ghana and Cote d'Ivoire.

Dear reader, I'm sharing with you history as has been told to me in the oral tradition. In fact, it is as if I've invited you to join me around a warm hearth on a moonlit night where, in rapt attention and with hands held together, we are being led into the lives of the first immigrants of Nkrankwanta, men and women who chose danger and uncertainty over servitude and complacency. It is the story of men and women who explored the unknown for new possibilities and opportunities, and who wanted their story to be told to generations after them. I am from Nkrankwanta and am privileged to be one of those entrusted with keeping alive the story of the *adikanfo*, or pace setters.

When my late granduncle Kwadwo Nziah decided it was time to pass on the story of the people to my generation through me, little did he know that I would one day share with the rest of the world what was then considered a family tradition. I don't know whether I have betrayed the confidence of my granduncle, but as long as telling the story will benefit wider society, I will apologize and take a bow at the same time.

Kwadwo Nziah was a preteen when my people migrated from their old town of Kotokoso to found a new one at Nkrankwanta. He had lived part of Anyii Kotoko history at Kotokoso in the French territory of Cote d'Ivoire and completed it at the founding of Nkrankwanta, in British Gold Coast. Kwadwo Nziah had also been told the history of his people before his time and generation, narrations that were etched in the spoken word as well as in the language of the talking drums.

Granduncle Nziah started out as a fetish priest and traditional healer. He became very knowledgeable about the curative properties of herbs, tree barks, and roots, for which he was sought after by patients from far and wide. As a royal from one of the two ruling houses of the Kotoko stool of Nkrankwanta, Kwadwo Nziah was already well versed in the history of Anyii Dwabene. But in the course of his travels to cure the sick and infirm, his appreciation for the customs, traditions, and history grew to include those of neighboring communities to Anyii Dwabene. Kwadwo Nziah was therefore a rich repository of knowledge when he decided to transmit to me the story of my people. And the fact Granduncle Nziah lived to well over one hundred years assures that he at least witnessed or lived through most of the events and circumstances that informed and shaped the history of Nkrankwanta.

Later in life, Kwadwo Nziah converted to Islam and took the name Ali. He even became the muezzin (caller to prayer) at the oldest mosque at Nkrankwanta. He also became *akyeamehene* (chief linguist) at the royal court of Anyii Kotoko at Nkrankwanta. It is Opanin Ali (Elder Ali), as many used to call him, who has imparted much of the information about the history of Nkrankwanta that I am sharing with you in this book. I could not have been better informed or learned from the feet of a more qualified teacher and mentor than Ali Kwadwo Nziah.

I have been fortunate in my information-gathering task because some of the narrators were eyewitnesses to events or had heard from parents and others who had lived the stories. The very fact I gathered information from people who either were the actors themselves or had listened to what took place directly from the mouths of the actors has improved the accuracy and truthfulness of what I have presented throughout these pages. Therefore, the probability of error, if any, has been minimal.

Regarding the history of Anyii Dwabene, I have drawn extensively from the groundbreaking fieldwork by the late Professor Koffi Sié, a son of Dwabene, which he submitted as dissertation toward his doctoral degree at the Université de Paris Pantheon–Sorbonne: "Les Agni-Diabè, Histoire et Societé." But across the continuum between the two family groups of Akan, namely Akan Twi-Fante and Akan Anyii-Baulé, I have relied on personal research and observation of contemporary Akan societies at play, both in Ghana and Cote d'Ivoire. I have also relied on the interpretation of the talking drums when they have codified events in history into few proverbial drumbeats.

The story of Anyii Dwabene, and for that matter Nkrankwanta, would not be complete without touching on the historical relationship with the larger Akan family in Ghana. I was raised and educated in Ghana. I believe that the fact I speak Twi as fluently as I speak Anyii Dwabene, my mother tongue, offers a huge advantage in the thorough appreciation of the cultural nuances of the two main branches of the greater Akan family, namely Akan Twi-Fante and Akan Anyii-Baulé. My education in Ghana included an extensive instruction in Akan history and the Twi language.

That Nkrankwanta was founded in 1917 and therefore is less than one hundred years old makes telling her story for the first time in the written word an enviable task. There is no doubt others will conduct further research in the future in order to write more about the story of Nkrankwanta, but being in the vanguard to elicit interest in further inquiry about a town that looks progressively different every two years from one's last visit is, to say the least, an opportunity no patriot or student of history can afford to pass up.

But one key reason I am publishing this book is to share information on the very origins of Nkrankwanta, with the view to educating those who may not know. By such a proactive approach, I hope to forestall some, if not all, of the common difficulties that have been associated with the institution of chieftaincy in Ghana, especially as they relate to succession and the bigger question of maintaining the peace. The truth is that as Nkrankwanta explodes in size and becomes an increasingly important town, some misinformed troublemaker may be tempted to disturb the peace by taking advantage of the lack of a written historical record. But when people have information that leads to knowledge, they tend to react rationally to issues and behave less violently, because for the most part, violence thrives on lies, and most lies thrive on ignorance. Nkrankwanta cannot afford to give up the uninterrupted peace and security it has enjoyed from the time its freedom-loving founders settled it in 1917.

Cultural Migration: A Short History of Nkrankwanta and Anyii Dwabene reminds of shared history and humanity, in the fact that the "Junction" welcomes and embraces all and offers unlimited opportunities in the realization of personal dreams. This book also draws inspiration from the mutual benefits improved relations among cultural communities along our common international borders can add to enhanced regional cooperation and, by extension, world peace.

The story of Nkrankwanta is essentially a story of migration. As such, it cannot be told in isolation of others who have been friends, collaborators, hosts, and guests. It is partly the story of a people who liberated others and, in turn, required assistance when they were faced with imminent danger. Again, the story of Nkrankwanta speaks to the human heart insofar as it portrays the changing fortunes in the lives of a people and, in this case, of a community that has seen a few relocations since from about 1670. Each step along the way has been purposeful, determined, with good intentions, rewarding, and with some luck. It is my belief and hope that all who show enough interest to continue through the rest of this book will come out with increased knowledge that will help them form a more informed and balanced opinion about Nkrankwanta and its founding culture.

Dear reader, by the time you turn the last page of this book, I hope to have informed you adequately enough about the success story that is Nkrankwanta. I invite you to join me on a journey—a historical journey that is still in the making.

AUTHOR'S NOTE

Throughout this book, I have presented as much as possible words, phrases, and object and place names in their proper and unique culture-specific forms and sounds. The aim is to ensure full, unadulterated meaning to subject and context.

In order to do this, I have adopted two special alphabetical characters unique to Akan phonetics. These are the vowels ɛ and ɔ. Phonetically, ɛ rhymes as in "ate," "get," "set," "bed," and so on. ɔ is the open o vowel in such English words as "awe," "got," "not," "pot," and so on.

Where I have written in Twi or Anyii, I have sometimes adopted the following letter combinations common with Twi: "ky" rendered in English as "tch," "gy" as in "dj," "dw" as in "djw", and "tw" as in "tchw." For example: "Kyebi," a town in southern Ghana, pronounces as "Tchebi"; "Agyekum," a common Akan male name, rhymes with "Adjekum"; "Twi," the main Akan language spoken in Ghana, pronounces as in "Tchwi"; and "Djwabene", as in Anyii Dwabene. Also, I have written "Anyii" as the name of an Akan tribe or people, where other writers have submitted Agni or Aowin.

Following is list of all twenty-two letters of Akan Twi-Fante alphabets:

a b d e ɛ f g h i k l m n o ɔ p r s t u w y

In order to fully accommodate Akan Anyii-Baulé languages and dialects, the letters *v* and *z* will need to be added to the list. That will make it an alphabetical list of twenty-four letters.

Chapter 1

The Name of a People

Anyii (French, Agni) is derived from "Bɛ wo yɛ, hene y'Anyi" (Twi, "Wɔwoo yɛn, na y'Anyin"). Roughly translated, Anyii means "We were precocious, even at birth."

In other words, the Anyii consider themselves a very levelheaded, civilized people.

The Anyii are a subgroup of the larger Akan ethnic group of tribes. Like all other Akan, the Anyii are matrilineal in heritage and traditional inheritance. In other words, primary lineage identification or accession to a throne is matrilineally defined and specific. Also, like all other Akan, the Anyii belong to the Kwa group of Niger-Congo languages.

Linguists, anthropologists, and ethnologists have struggled with Akan language classification. While all seem to agree that Asante, Akwapem, Bono, Akyem, and related tribes and dialects belong to the Twi strand of Akan, many among them disagree Fante qualifies in the classification of Twi, even though speakers of either language have no difficulty understanding each other.

On the other hand, there is near unanimity regarding Anyii-Baulé as the other group of Akan languages and dialects. Of this, the major languages include Anyii, Baulé, Nzema, Sefwi, Wassa, and Ahanta.

Emmanuel Nicholas Abakah of the Department of Akan-Nzema, University of Winneba, Ghana, has provided a very interesting analysis of Akan language groups. Because of the inclusiveness and comprehensiveness of this study, I am persuaded to classify Akan languages under two main groups, namely Twi-Fante, and Anyii-Baulé. Under each group are some of the following languages:

1. Twi-Fante comprises Asante, Bono, Akwamu, Adanse, Assin, Akyem, Denkyira, Akwapem, Fante, Kwahu, etc.
2. Anyii-Baulé: Anyii, Baulé, Esahié (Sefwi), Esuma (Nzema), Wassa, Ahanta, Atché, Bonouan, etc.

The Anyii language includes ten dialects, namely Sanvi, Indenie, Dwabene (Djuablin), Mɔrɔnou (Mɔrɔ fo), Annɔ, Bini, Bɔnaa, Barebɔ, Abɛɛ, and Alangua. Probably, the Anyii constitute the fourth largest tribal group in Cote d'Ivoire and make up a small percentage of Akan in Ghana. Anyii in Ghana are concentrated mainly along the Ghana-Cote d'Ivoire border in the Western Region, and in a few towns to the southwestern tip of Brong Ahafo Region.

Almost all Twi-speaking Akan live in Ghana, while roughly 70 percent of Anyii-Baulé Akan call Cote d'Ivoire home. Even so, all Ivorian Akan, with the exception of Abron Bonduku, migrated from modern-day south-central Ghana as separate groups, and over a span of some two centuries, beginning in the seventeenth century. Major causes of migration are reported to have included family feuds, sibling rivalry and competition, internal conflicts over the right to rule, expansionist campaigns of neighboring groups, and territorial control. There is no recorded history of Akan migration from the heartland of present-day Ghana for reasons of economics or as a direct result of the transatlantic slave trade.

Recent census figures put Akans at a little over 47 (47.3) percent of the total population of Ghana. In Cote d'Ivoire, Akan constitute about 42 percent of the total population. Asante in Ghana, and Baulé in Cote d'Ivoire, each represent the single largest Akan tribe, respectively. Chokosi is a small Akan group in northern Togo whose members are believed to have migrated from Anyii Annɔ in Cote d'Ivoire. The Chokosi refer to themselves as Annɔfoɛ (Twi: Annɔ foɔ), or "People from Annɔ."

The Anyii inhabit land that stretches in a north-south direction between the edges of the Savannah in Cote d'Ivoire, immediately south of Bonduku, and the estuaries of the Bia and Tano, just before the two rivers drain their waters into the Atlantic Ocean. On an east-west axis, the Anyii share borders with the Baulé, a closely related Akan group, to the west. To the east, the Anyii are neighbors with the following major groups: Dormaa, Esahié (Sefwi), Atché, and Nzema. Dormaa and Esahie are entirely in Ghana, while Nzema, like the Anyii, are split between Ghana and Cote d'Ivoire. Notable Anyii towns include Abengourou (Ampenkro), AnyiniBilékro, Aboisso, Krindjabo, Bongouanou, Ngala Ngwandaa (Nkrankwanta), Dadieso, Elubo (Elui-bo; Dui-ase or Odum-ase), and Angyé (Enchi). The last three towns are located in the Western Region of Ghana. Ngala Nwandwaa is in Brong Ahafo. The Comoe, Nzi, Tano, and Bia are the four major rivers that course through Anyii territory, with Comoe being the largest.

Anyii Dwabene shares borders with the following major traditional areas: Abron (Bonduku) to the north; Anyii-Bonaa to the northeast; Anyii-Bini to the west; Anyii-Indenie to the south; Anyii-Mɔrɔfo to the southwest; Esahié (Sefwi) to the southeast; and Dormaa to the east.

All Anyii Dwabene towns are located in Cote d'Ivoire, with the exception of Ngala Ngwandaa (Nkrankwanta), the central subject of this book. Also deserving mention is the fact that Ngala Ngwandaa shares in its vicinity other Anyii towns. However, Yaakro (formerly Senikro), Kofi Badukro, Atosikro, Gonokro, Kofi Kumikro, and a few other Anyii towns located in the same Dormaa traditional area as Ngala Ngwadaa are of Anyii-Bonaa extraction.

Chapter 2

Migration from Amansie

Nantefo (The Sojourners)

They walk in the thoughts of their woes,
When out of unfairness and greed,
Kindred behaved like a true foe,
Relentless in greed and deceit.
But in subdued angst, they preferred peace,
Wherefore they chose to leave the fold.

Knowing where not a new place to call home
But with steady hands and courage unmatched,
They embraced the tortuous challenge
To catch onto something of hope.

Bearing in mind the unknown destiny by the Creator,
Perchance they land on something greater.

Zac Adama

The sojourners prod on in earnest,
In steely resolve, firm and sure.
Their closest companion was silence,
Which they bore with patience.

Failure they contemplated not to bear,
For they desired not a return to the rear,
A past not amenable to repair.

They press on toward an unknown destination,
Which destiny may ordain as a new nation.

Perchance they'll emerge waxed like the moon,
Or the attempt'll frustrate cherished aspirations
And turn a pleasant dream into painful doom.

From a vantage, their semblance is the oriental star
    of dawn,
Lolling up to sew the past darkness of garments torn
Or to be tossed into the turbulence of cascading sea
    waves,
Wherefore they struggle even to be swept ashore.
The effort will provide material for a few generations,
Fodder sufficient to feed a grand jury of public
    opinion.
For the gossip as well as the genuine raconteur,
Material worth the storyteller's wise narration
Or the fool's undeserved condemnation.

Along the way to the abyss,
They found companionship among fleeing Denkyira,
Hackneyed, bruised, and stressed to the hilt.
In defeat, the decisive battle at Feyiase, 'twas
At the hands of unsuspecting Asante.

The pinnacle of a war that rearranged a relationship
Whence overlord switched places with subordinate.
A veritable lesson that time is in a perpetual motion,
In a flux and endless permutable arrangement,
Metamorphosis of role-play only time herself can tell.

Empathy and love they found among the Sahié,
In the manner of long-lost siblings found.
Warm and friendly hosts, those brethren!
But the "Nantefo" must needs press on,
Lest the sun set on lofty hopes and aspirations.

New life begins at Dadieso.
The sojourners, a nation with many lessons learned,
To uphold fairness, patience, and firmness,
Sharing, content with self and friendship with
    neighbors.
Anyii, they were mature even at birth, a name
    befitting.

Some historians believe the Anyii Dwabene left
their former home in Amansie in present-day Ghana
around 1697. It is more likely the migration took place

earlier. What is certain is that the Anyii Dwabene left Amansie before the founding of Asanteman, or the Nation of Asante, when several groups of smaller kingdoms formed a military alliance to defeat and rid themselves of political control from the powerful kingdom of Denkyira at the decisive Battle of Feyiase in 1701.

Several francophone researchers and oral historians in Cote d'Ivoire have referred to a place called Assuamara or Assuémara, north of Dankira whence the Anyii Dwabene migrated. No doubt, the place names are distortions of Asumegya, which is north of the once-powerful kingdom of Denkyira. For example, Koffi Sié cites Maurice Delafosse as source and authority regarding the Anyii Dwabene having migrated from Assuamara or Assuémara in 1697 as the direct result of the assassination of "Obiri Ebwa" by one "Kwasi, chief of Odomara." There is little doubt Delafosse's account of that event relates more to the assassination of Obiri Yeboah, chief of Kumase (1660–80) by the Dormaa (Odomara), who then lived at Asumegya. The entire Dwaben group, before it split into two and later three distinct states, lived next-door in the territory of Amansie. The three Dwaben states are: Anyii Dwabene (Anyinibilekro, Cote d'Ivoire), Asante Dwaben (Dwaben, Ghana), and New Dwaben (Koforidua, Ghana). Each state is independent of the other.

Another account has it that the leader of the group that broke away as Anyii Dwabene, one Kwasi, lost out to another candidate in a chieftaincy contest. Feeling cheated and angry, Kwasi left with his followers to go establish a kingdom of their own. The fact that Kwasi could commandeer a group large enough to go form a new nation somewhere suggests not only was he a royal but a powerful and highly respected one.

A critical analysis of the two versions about why the Anyii Dwabene left their original home tilts the balance in favor of a disappointed Kwasi departing with his followers to go found a new kingdom. For, if Anyii Dwabene had had a hand in or had been suspected of having had knowledge of the assassination of Obiri Yeboah, it would seem unreasonable to have waited some seventeen years (1680–97) before considering escaping from certain retribution from Osei Tutu, who not only succeeded his uncle Obiri Yeboah but founded the powerful Asante kingdom. As a matter of fact, there is no historical account to the effect Anyii Dwabene and Asante ever engaged in skirmishes or went to war.

Further, knowing the Asante as a rather warlike lot, they would not have hesitated shooting a few ballistics in the direction of those they suspected had had a hand in the murder of their popular chief of Kumase, namely Nana Obiri Yeboah. The fact the group that later called itself Anyii Dwabene has no historical account of war between it and Asante is sufficient proof the latter did not suspect the former in the assassination of Obiri Yeboah. After all, the name Asante is derived from "Sa-Nti" (Because of War), when a few otherwise disorganized and weak paramountcies came together to form a united and strong fighting force in order to rid themselves of Denkyira hegemony. It is therefore reasonable to conclude that Amansie Kwasi and his Anyii Dwabene people did not migrate on account of the assassination of Nana Obiri Yeboah, Kumasehene (chief of Kumase).

It is more likely Kwasi and his followers left Dwaben in Amansie earlier than 1697. The migration could have happened in or about 1670, at the beginning of the reign of Nana Adarkwa Yiadom, the first Dwabenhene (king of a united Dwaben state), who ruled from 1670 to 1715. Since Anyii Dwabene left Amansie as a result of their leader losing in a contest to be chief, rather than as a result of the killing of Nana Obiri Yeboah, Kumasehene, it is reasonable to say that Kwasi lost the chieftaincy bid to no other person than Nana Adarkwa Yiadom, first Dwabenhene. And Anyii Dwabene had long left the crib by the time Asante was founded in 1701. The chronological analysis leaves the year 1670 as the last date Kwasi and Anyii Dwabene could have reasonably been present in Amansie.

Kwasi and his followers left Amansie because they had been cheated out of a chieftaincy role. Though disappointed, they preferred exodus to confrontation and perhaps civil war. Interestingly, a group in Ghana that calls itself Asante Dwaben (and by extension New Dwaben, a breakaway group from Asante Dwaben) traces its origins to the Amansie area about the same time as Kwasi and his people were there. With such close similarities in historical origins, it is reasonable to say that Anyii Dwabene and the two Dwaben groups in Ghana (Asante Dwaben and New Dwaben) are related. But unlike Anyii Dwabene, Asante Dwaben became a member of the Asante Confederacy and played several key roles in the wars and decisions that shaped the kingdom and empire. The confederacy was unlike a federation because each senior member was an autonomous nation that was under no obligation to join and thus could leave the union at will. Asante Dwaben is an autonomous member of the Asante Confederacy, which is now called Asanteman.

In both Asante Dwaben and Anyii Dwabene, references have been made that suggest each side is aware of the blood relationship between them. For example, a blogger by the name Akrase, a son of Asante Dwaben, writes as follows: "In fact, Dwabens aren't situate (sic) in Ghana only. In La Cote d'Ivoire, they can be found in large nos., in Assikasou."

Later in this book, I will inform that the first capital of Anyii Dwabene was Asikaso, before King Anyini Bilé moved it to Anyini-Bilé-Kro, his plantation, in 1880. Asikaso still exists as a small town near AnyiniBilékro, a shadow of its old grandeur and political significance.

Some Anyii Dwabene have made references to their old home of New Dwaben. While the location and point of reference cannot be accurate since New Juaben state was founded about 1875, almost two centuries after the founding of Anyii Dwabene in

1750, there nevertheless exists mutual knowledge and awareness between Anyii Dwabene and her Dwaben blood relatives in Ghana, and vice versa.

It is estimated that Kwasi and his half of Dwaben (that is, Anyii Dwabene) left Amansie in 1670, a few years before the founding of the Asante Confederacy, following the defeat of King Ntim Gyakari of Denkyira at the Battle of Feyiase in 1701. Asante Dwaben, on the other hand, became a founding member of Asante and the confederacy. But in 1832, Asante attacked Dwaben over suspicions the latter had collaborated with the enemy in the battle of Akatamanso in which the Asante army, for the first time, lost to the coastal states and their British allies. Nana Kwaku Boateng, the Dwaben king and several followers, took refuge in Akyem Abuakwa in south-central Ghana. In 1841, reconciliation was struck at a meeting at Kumase between Asante (the confederacy) and Dwaben (an autonomous member of the confederacy).

However, in 1875–76 and for the second time, the Dwaben returned as refugees to Akyem Abuakwa. Asante had attacked Dwaben one more time following the former's loss to the British in the Sagrenti War of 1873–74. Historians have named that war after Major-General Sir Garnet Wolseley (Sagrenti, or Sir Garnet), who commanded the British Army. The Sagrenti War was the third of five so-called Anglo-Ashanti wars. It seemed that each time Asante lost in a major war, leaders in Kumase suspected Dwaben collaboration with the enemy. Perhaps Asante had reason to doubt Dwaben loyalty to the cause of the confederacy. Be as it may, the Dwaben refugees wanted to live in permanent peace. This time around, they were joined by other Asante refugees from Afigyaase and Asokore.

In the second Dwaben exodus to Akyem Abuakwa, the refugees decided to establish a permanent home, which they named New Dwaben. New Dwaben towns include Koforidua, Effiduase (Afigyaase), and Asokore. Dwaben (old) is still in Asante, while New Dwaben is in the southeast toward Accra, in the Eastern Region of Ghana. Of the three Dwaben(e) kingdoms, namely Asante Dwaben, Anyii Dwabene, and New Dwaben, Nkrankwanta from Anyii Dwabene, and the entire New Dwaben, live on land belonging to traditional authorities other than their own. Nkrankwanta is situated on land belonging to Dormaaman, while New Dwaben territory is land originally owned by Akyem Abuakwa. This is due to their respective peculiar circumstances as refugees.

Following the fall of Denkyira at the hands of Osei Tutu at the Battle of Feyiase in 1701, a significant number of fleeing Denkyira joined the ranks of Amansie Kwasi and his people on the flanks of Esahié (Sefwi) territory and assimilated into the new Anyii Dwabene tribe. Together, they settled at Dadieso in present-day Western Region of Ghana. Old Denkyira broke into many parts as a direct result of their defeat at the hands of Osei Tutu, founder of Asante. A piece of Denkyira hanged on at Jukwa, Dunkwa, and in other towns, but a significant number of Denkyira natives metamorphosed or merged into other tribes, such as Wassa, Esahié (Sefwi), and Anyii.

The emigrants traversed Esahié (Sefwi) territory and finally settled at Dadieso in what is now the Western Region of Ghana and called themselves Anyii Dwabene. It is possible Anyii Dwabene founded Dadieso, cofounded it with another group, or were accorded significant founder role by earlier settlers of the town. The fact that a few decades following their arrival the Amansie immigrants were already exercising political power and authority and making far-reaching decisions is evidence the Anyii Dwabene had significant influence. An example of significant political power and authority was when an emissary from Abron Bonduku was sent to Dadieso to seek military assistance so an embattled kingdom of Abron could be saved and restored. The recognition of Anyii Dwabene becomes more significant, considering the request for assistance came from one of the oldest and most resourced Akan states at the time and of all time. The fact Abron Bonduku bypassed so many neighboring states in the region and sought military assistance and protection from the Anyii Dwabene at Dadieso to the far south is enough evidence the Dwabene developed a well-organized political and military system within the relatively short time since arriving at Dadieso.

Assuming further that an earlier group had settled Dadieso prior to the arrival of Kwasi and his followers, it would be reasonable to suggest that just as did Abron Bonduku a few decades later, these earlier settlers must have readily welcomed the immigrants from Amansie and Denkyira for the military protection the latter would provide them. In this regard, it is easy to understand why an earlier group at Dadieso would gladly and readily share political power and, in some respects, defer to or even cede critical state decision making to a stronger new group. It is as well probable that given their numbers, but more importantly their relatively stronger military presence, the Anyii Dwabene asked of their hosts, if existed, a significant stake in state affairs.

It is important to underscore early on that Anyii Dwabene did not conquer to rule at Dadieso, assuming there were earlier settlers or founders. If they met earlier residents, it is very likely the immigrants from Amansie negotiated their way into a position of prominence and eventually, dominance. In any event, the Anyii Dwabene became significantly influenced by neighboring states, notably the Esahié (Sefwi). Evidence of this influence is the common worship of the river god "Soborε," an Esahié deity. Beside the worship of the god, Soborε entered into Anyii Dwabene cultural repertoire and collection of names. For example, one of the earliest queen mothers of Nkrankwanta was Nana Ama Soborε.

NANA AMA SƆBORƆ QUEEN MOTHER OF
RANKWANTA DIED ON

Nana Ama Soborɛ, late queen mother of Nkrankwanta

The power and importance of Soborɛ has been recorded by one historian, himself a son of Esahié (Sefwi). In his work, *The History of My People (Sefwi)*, K.Y. Daaku writes, "The three states of Sefwi share a common culture in spite of the fact that they all came from different places ... In the worship of the tutelar deity Soborɛ, the three states also have a common identity. The deity is supposed not only to protect the states from all calamities but it is also a fertility god."

Anyii Dwabene is sometimes called Anyii Diabe. The name origin of Diabe is unclear. A good guess would be that it is a nick-name, perhaps derived from the Twi words "Di Abɛ" ("consumers of palm products," or even "palm wine drinkers"). This group of Anyii, however, prefers to be called Dwabene (misrepresented as Djablin or Djuablin by the French colonialists).

Chapter 3

War between Bouna and Abron Bonduku

Around 1750, war broke out between the states of Bouna and Abron (Bonduku). Bouna had invaded Abron, and the latter was struggling to fight back and dislodge her bellicose neighbor from occupied territory. It is said that when the king of Bonduku consulted with his council of elders and high priests about the way forward, he was informed about a people called Anyii Dwabene who lived a few days' journey to the south of his kingdom, at a place called Dadieso. According to the oral historical account of this event, the high priest of Abron advised his king that it was with the help of Anyii Dwabene that he would gain victory over the Bouna aggressor and enemy. The Abron king at the time is believed to have been Nana Kofi Sono, who ruled from 1746 to 1760. So the king sent an emissary to the chiefs of Dadieso to request military assistance, as had been divined by the high priest and with the consent of his council of elders.

After careful review of the request by the messengers from the king of Abron and background information to the conflict, the chiefs and elders of Dadieso concluded that Bouna was aggressor. On that account, the royal court of Dadieso decided to commit warriors to liberate a fellow Akan state under attack. The consent of Dadieso to help restore territory, rights, and pride to Abron was purely on humanitarian and altruistic grounds. There was no quid pro quo agreement, nor a contractual requirement to pay a specified sum of money, value in gold, or other valuable asset as prior condition to help liberate Abron Bonduku. Even in the absence of a formal agreement of a political or military alliance, it was common practice in those days that a people or kingdom would join a conflict or war on the side of a friendly neighbor or more, if there was a common blood relationship or common history. In the case of Bouna against Abron Bonduku, Dadieso accepted to assist a fellow Akan state under attack.

It is significant to note that prior to the Bouna-Abron War, Dadieso and Bonduku had had no special relationship, nor were they in any form of political or military alliance. It is very likely that any relationship between the two was perfunctory, no more than the knowledge that the other existed. Or at a different level where citizens from either kingdom would occasionally meet at one of the trading centers of the day, each engaged in private commercial activity.

However, the successful rescue mission by the Anyii Dwabene warriors created a permanent relationship and fraternity between the two Akan groups, a bond that is as strong today as it was in 1750.

The contingent that left Dadieso comprised a few dozen warriors. Their logistics consisted of enough food and water for a few days, expecting to replenish supplies in the nutritionally fecund and fertile landscape between Dadieso and Bonduku. They travelled light and fast. It is further related that the logistics for the expedition included seven guns and sufficient gunpowder to last for a few months of battle. The Anyii fighting force was made up of veterans of earlier wars in Amansie and Denkyira as well as skilled big-game hunters and marksmen. The company of warriors was placed under the command of Bredu Asamandje, a brave veteran of earlier wars in Amansie and a very experienced fusilier and big-game hunter. The order to the expedition was to liberate Abron Bonduku and return to Dadieso.

After several days through known forest pathways, the Dadieso warriors emerged into the semi Savannah northern part of Abron territory and ultimately, Bonduku, the royal capital, where they were ushered into the presence of Nana Kofi Sono, king of Abron, and their host. The following day, the king, sitting in state with his council of elders and top military advisors, including the Safohene (chief of defense staff) briefed Bredu Asamandje and his visiting warriors about the mission for which they had sought their assistance. The Dwabene fighters were provided with all necessary information about the war, including intelligence reports about the relative size and strength of the enemy. Intelligence reports also included names and known capabilities of key enemy field commanders, type and level of sophistication of weapons, military formation, and, most importantly, enemy location. Having obtained all information necessary for battle, the Dwabene warriors took a few days of needed rest, familiarized themselves with the terrain, and mapped out a strategy. They were to be assisted by local Abron fighters who knew the territory thoroughly well and could be trusted to relay messages back and forth between battlefield activity and the leadership of Abron at Bonduku. A few locals were also assigned rear-guard duty as porters and support staff. The warriors from Dadieso were ready for battle.

One account of the war has it that the Dwabene fighters came upon flocks of wild birds, most probably doves or hornbills, foraging in the undergrowth. Knowing the Bouna fighters were within earshot, the Dwabene forces would deliberately shoot into the air, disturbing and scaring off as many as possible the wild fowls. As the frightened birds noisily took to the air and in all directions, they gave the impression of an approaching large army of infantrymen. Believing they were outnumbered and outgunned, the Bouna warriors took to their heels, homeward bound.

Another battlefield account of the same war has a magical twist to it and leaves little room for rational or verifiable deductive analysis. About this version, when the Dwabene warriors entered the battlefield, they invoked one of the guardian gods of Anyii Dwabene by calling, "Akaa éé! Akaa éé!" And with each invocation, several *kaka tikaa* or gnomes (*mmoatia* in Twi) would appear, armed and in surrogate battle readiness. So the call to arms on the plains of Abron Bonduku, according to this version of war correspondence, was that kaka tikaa (short spirits) or gnomes did the actual fighting.

Elsewhere in this book, I have mentioned that Anyii Kotoko migrated to Nkrankwanta both in the physical and spiritual senses. There, I mentioned that the spiritual migration involved the Bia Bilé, or sacred stool, and performing gods, two of whom I introduced as Soborɛ, the river god of fertility, and Nzolɛ, the protector and warrior god. Soborɛ is female, while Nzolɛ is male. Of Nzolɛ, I mentioned that he goes by the nickname Akaa Akomea and manifests as a kaka tikaa or gnome when it chooses to be seen. So on the battlefield on the plains of Abron Bonduku in 1750, there are those who attribute victory to the spiritual intervention of the god Nzolɛ.

In both accounts of the war, three events stand out: there was easy victory that did not necessitate a significant loss of life, if at all; victory was won through the agency of clever tactics the Anyii Dwabene fighters adopted by placing third-party nonhuman agents between themselves and Bouna enemy lines (a flock of birds or an army of angry little gnomes); and a common agreement that a multitude of objects (birds or gnomes) frightened the enemy into desertion and ultimate victory for Anyii Dwabene warriors.

For giving up the fight so easily without the least resistance, one can infer from the two versions of report on the war that the fighters of Bouna either had inferior arms (perhaps no more than bows and arrows) or lacked in war technique, strategy, and discipline. Fear and even cowardice may be adduced for how quickly Bouna fighters showed their heels on the plains of Bonduku—fear to meet up with a hyped Anyii Dwabene fighting force. An important lesson that can be drawn from the 1750 war between Bouna and Abron Bonduku is that except for occasional skirmishes, the war ended all wars between the two neighbors. Therefore, it is recorded history to say that warriors from Dadieso restored and saved the kingdom of Abron at a crucial time in her history. For that, Abron Bonduku has been eternally grateful to Anyii Dwabene.

After victory, an elated king of Bonduku offered the Dadieso warriors ownership of the uninhabited southern flank of his vast kingdom in gratitude. Nana Kofi Sono also reasoned that Dwabene as a next-door neighbor would assure security to his kingdom and people. But the Dwabene warriors thanked him and insisted on returning to their Dadieso home to the south instead. On the return journey home, the warriors decided to camp on the shores of River Baaso, for needed rest and to restock their provisions for the remaining leg of the journey back to Dadieso. It was there they discovered gold in the riverbed beneath the clear waters of River Baaso and along its banks. The warriors decided to suspend the trip back to Dadieso and instead founded a settlement they named Sikaa-So (Place of Gold, or Goldfields), which later became Asikaso, in reference to the rich gold (*sikaa*) field they had just discovered and intended to mine. The year was still 1750.

Chapter 4

A New Nation Is Born

Naturally, Asikaso became the capital of the new kingdom, with Bredu Asamandje, leader of the military contingent to Abron, becoming the first king of Anyii Dwabene. In no time, the population of Asikaso was bolstered by a large migration of Anyii Dwabene from Dadieso. Notable among the first immigrants from Dadieso were the following females of royal lineage: Asamala Dehyeε, Somala, and Seala. It is no surprise, therefore, that Asamala, Somala, and Seala have remained popular girl child names among Anyii Dwabene.

As the population grew, other settlements were founded around Asikaso. Among the first Anyii Dwabene towns, beside Asikaso, were (in random order) Dame, Kotokoso, and Dokaanu. As the first historical town between Abron Bonduku and Anyii Dwabene, Dokaanu plays the role of a gateway stop of sorts.

In recognition of the special relationship between

Abron Bonduku and Anyii Dwabene but more importantly the fact the former is host, Dwabene offered deference to Abron in the celebration of the annual Eluedié yam festival. In other words, Abron celebrates its yam festival before Dwabene does.

In most African societies where farming is a major occupational pursuit, there is an annual festival to officially usher in the harvest of the main food crop or produce of the land or waterways, such as grain, climbers, root crops, or seafood. In the specific example of Abron and Dwabene, yams have a special place among food crops. An annual tradition in the two states and among several others in the subregion, the overlord or king presides over an elaborate ceremony to perform specific customary rites to officially declare open the harvest season. In recognition of the special historical bond between them, Abron Bonduku and Anyii Dwabene have since 1750 been assisting each other to celebrate the occasion with a powerful contingent of royal court representation bearing gifts and messages of fraternity. The celebration of the respective yam festivals reminds of a period in history when Anyii Dwabene proved she was a true and trusted friend in a time of need, and a reliable ally Abron Bonduku was privileged to have and keep within sight.

Another aspect of the deep relationship between Abron and Dwabene is that in the event of a dispute, misunderstanding, or protracted litigation between individuals, communities, or towns among Anyii Dwabene, the intervention of a chief of Abron must resolve the difficulty at hand. Under such circumstances, the mediation of a chief of Abron or his assign must put to rest the misunderstanding, anger, animosity, or even hatred between the parties. The same is also true if the peace must be maintained between feuding parties among the Abron. The parties simply embrace and make up, regardless how difficult the situation or high the stakes. They do so not out of fear of authority or punitive repercussion but in deference to the deep friendship and respect that has governed relationships between Abron and Dwabene since 1750. In effect, Abron and Dwabene stand up for each other, both in times of war and peace. There is also an unwritten code or convention that forbids fighting between Abron and Dwabene. There is no better foreign relations policy or friendlier neighborliness!

Bredu Asamandje became the first king of Anyii Dwabene, with capital at Asikaso. But in 1880, Anyini Bilé I (the seventh occupant of the Anyii Dwabene stool) moved the capital from Asikaso to his plantation at Anyini-Bilé-Kro (Anyini Bilé Town). The Dwabene royal capital, which is now a significant administrative and commercial town in Cote d'Ivoire, appears on maps as Agniblékro, or even Agniblékrou, a clear misrepresentation of a people's culture!

There are two ruling houses to the Anyii Dwabene paramount stool at Agniblékro: the Asikasofoɛ, or House of Asikaso (direct descendants of Bredu Asamandje), and the Dadiesofoɛ, or House of Dadieso (royals from Dadieso who migrated to join kith and kin, following the founding of Asikaso and the state of Anyii Dwabene in 1750).

Following is complete list of Anyii Dwabene Brembi (Twi: Amanhene) or kings:

YY	Name	Tenure	Royal Capital	Comments
1.	Bredu Asamandje	From 1750	Asikaso	From the royal House of Asikaso. Was field commander of warriors who left Dadieso to liberate Abron Bonduku from Bouna invasion.
2.	Asemia Kwadjane		Asikaso	Bredu's younger brother (House of Asikaso).
3.	Kpanyi Kwame		Asikaso	Appointed directly by kingmakers of Dadieso. Hence, the royal House of Dadieso.
4.	Ekyea Kwasi		Asikaso	House of Dadieso.
5.	Awia Kotoki (a.k.a., Awia Kpanyi)		Asikaso	House of Dadieso.
6.	Kofi Nango	Died 1880	Asikaso	House of Asikaso. Kofi Nango was chief of Yobouakro immediately before his elevation as king of Dwabene.
7.	Anyini Bilé I	1880–1890	Agniblékro	House of Asikaso. Succeeded his father, Kofi Nango. Evidence his mother was, as father, of royal lineage and cousins. His reign coincided with the arrival of French colonialism to Dwabene.

| 8. | Yaw Fum | 1890–1898 | Tengualan | House of Dadieso. Founder of Tengualan. Yaw Fum ruled from Tengualan, arguing that AnyiniBilékro, the new Dwabene capital, deserved better than to be situated on a plantation owned by Anyini Bilé, his predecessor, who it is said he didn't like very much. Yaw Fum, prior to becoming Dwabene king, had arrived from Dadieso and risen to become a notable rubber collector. The French executed him by firing squad, along with Nanou (chief of Manzanouan) and Boadu (chief of Nyandaa, a.k.a. Boadukro), after losing the 1898 uprising to uproot French presence in Dwabene, a.k.a. the War of Asikaso. This sad incident in Dwabene history is remembered as Alaka Nza (the Three Coffins), the Dwabene state oath, in sad memory of the coffins containing the bodies of the three executed Dwabene traditional rulers. Also, the 1898 conquest set French colonialism firmly on Dwabene territory. |

9.	Awia Kwaw (a.k.a. Awia Famea)	1898–1916	Agniblékro	House of Asikaso.
10.	Kwabana Ayisi	1916–1920	Agniblékro	House of Dadieso. Was chief of Tengualan immediately prior to becoming king of Dwabene. A descendant of Yaw Fum.
11.	Alu Manlan	1920–1920	Agniblékro	House of Asikaso. Was king for only a few days, replaced by Ndaa Kwasi, on charges of laziness, incompetence, and a poor custodian of royal assets.
12,	Ndaa Kwasi	1920–1934	Agniblékro	House of Asikaso. First educated Dwabene king. Replaced Alu Manlan. Ndaa Kwasi was preferred by the French colonial administration, ostensibly because he was educated.
13.	Kwaw Bilé	1934–1982	Agniblékro	House of Asikaso. Converted to Islam while on the throne.
14.	Rule by Regency	1982–1984	Agniblékro	No substantive king.

15.	Anyini Bilé II	1984– Present	Agniblékro	House of Asikaso. Holds a doctorate in law and was a career diplomat (last posting was as ambassador of Cote d'Ivoire to Central African Republic) from where he was called home to ascend the Dwabene throne.

The Three Original Stools of Anyii Dwabene

The state of Anyii Dwabene was founded in 1750, when warriors from Dadieso, having accomplished their mission to liberate Abron Bonduku from Bouna invasion, reconsidered an earlier offer to settle on Abron land following the discovery of gold in and around River Baaso, at what was later named Asikaso, which also became the first royal capital.

The most important symbol of the new state, in accordance with Akan political organization and usage, is the carving and purification of the sacred stool, the Bia Bilé, or Black Stool. In Akan traditional system and lore, a darkened wooden stool at once represents the collective soul of the people and serves as source of highest political authority. Because it is the primordial source of power and point of reference, the Black Stool sometimes conjures an aura and significance of earthly godhead. The shining blackness of the stool is the result of accumulated sacrificial animal blood and other objects over time. An Akan tribe, kingdom, or town is as old as its founding Black Stool.

The chief or king does not sit on the Bia Bilé, except on special occasions like the day of his coronation. Even then, the rite associated with the coronation is limited to a brief, touch-and-go seating on the ancient stool. This piece of the coronation ceremony is performed away from public view. Beside the Black Stool, the next most important object of political authority among the Akan is the state sword, often carved with a gilded handle, which an incoming chief or king holds to swear fealty and allegiance to his people.

A mounted Akan state sword; note the gold-gilded handle.
At coronation ceremony, a new chief holds it in his right
hand to swear allegiance to the people and the stool he is
about to ascend. The state sword is a symbol of authority.

In the case of Anyii Dwabene, when the state stool was carved, two supporting stools were also carved from the same piece of wood—namely that of Kotokoso (later Nkrankwanta) and Dame, in that order. It is said that Kotokoso (now Nkrankwanta) passed on the piece of wood immediately after that for Asikaso (the state stool at Anyiniblekro, which was carved out of the base of the wood) to Dame on account it was crooked. That decision was taken for no other reason than preferred taste and esthetics on the part of Nkrankwanta. It therefore did not negate, diminish, or rearrange the relative seniority among the three stools or towns of Anyii Dwabene state. In what may be called "The Triple Crown Heritage," the significance of the first three Anyii Dwabene stools, coming one after the other from the same piece of wood, represents the relative seniority and importance each royal stool enjoys in the political hierarchy of the state of Anyii Dwabene. The three stools coming from the same piece of wood also symbolize an inseparable bond and relationship, one to the other. Recognition of this relationship has remained unbroken since the very birth of Anyii Dwabene in 1750.

The relationship between the paramount stool of Agniblékro (formerly at Asikaso) and those of Nkrankwanta (formerly at Kotokoso) and Dame is similar to that of a set of triplets, with Agniblékro as eldest brother. Therefore, Agniblékro, Nkrankwanta, and Dame are the primary stools at the very heart of Anyii Dwabene statehood. Although the different colonial heritage may have somewhat affected this relationship, especially from the point of view that Nkrankwanta is in Anglophone Ghana while the rest of Anyii Dwabene towns are located in Francophone Cote d'Ivoire, the geographical isolation has not dented the importance of Nkrankwanta to her Dwabene umbilical chord and shared history with Anyiniblekro, Dame, and the other towns. Another significant aspect of the relationship between Kotoko (Nkrankwanta) and Agniblékro is that Nkrankwanta celebrates its Eluedié (yam festival) the same day as Agniblékro.

Tengualan ranks as another senior member in the state hierarchy, by virtue of the fact that its stool and other royal paraphernalia came directly from Dadieso, the immediate ancestral home of the Anyii Dwabene. This fact underscores the unbroken link and bond between Anyii Dwabene and Dadieso. Equally instructive is the fact that Yaw Fum, founder and first chief of Tengualan, became the eighth king of Anyii Dwabene in 1890. Not only had Yaw Fum emigrated from the Anyii royal house at Dadieso, he had been sent to Dwabene with a stool and other royal paraphernalia, ostensibly to drum home the point that Dadieso considered Dwabene an extension of its kingdom. Or, more pointedly, to complement the throne created for Bredu Asamandje. In fact, Dadieso had earlier directly interfered in the affairs of Anyii Dwabene when it appointed Kpanyi Kwame as third king.

Consequently, the Dadiesofoɛ, or ruling house

of Dadieso in Dwabene had, in the past, considered themselves truer royalty than the Asikasofoɛ, or House of Asikaso who, at the back of their mind, were not royals in the proper sense since Bredu Asamandje, their patriarch, was a warrior under orders of true royalty at Dadieso. Therefore, Dadieso had reasoned and perhaps continues to reason that Bredu, and by extension his direct descendants, have elevated themselves beyond their proper station in Dwaben society. This state of affairs, though subdued, continues to play itself out as evidenced by the lesser than warm relationship between Agniblékro and Dadieso, especially when the Dwabene monarch has been from the House of Asikaso. Perhaps also, this explains why Yaw Fum (from the House of Dadieso) is alleged to have never really liked or respected Anyini Bilé (from the House of Asikaso), his immediate predecessor. It is reasonable to believe that at the back of his mind, Yaw Fum never regarded Anyini Bilé royal enough to be king of all of Anyii Dwabene.

Chapter 5

War of Asikaso: April 29–July 2, 1898

The War of Asikaso lasted exactly sixty-four days, when Anyii Dwabene warriors staged an uprising that was destined to fail because of poor, uncoordinated war strategy and political acumen against a sophisticated world political and military power. French colonial influence over Anyii Dwabene was virtually nonexistent until about 1880 and during the reign of King Anyini Bilé I. Even by then, contact between the colonial and traditional administrations was one of mutual curiosity and courteous regard of each other. This relationship, however, was to make a radical change in a relatively short time.

By 1880, the Anyii Dwabene economy depended almost entirely on the rubber trade, with limited contribution from gold mining. Later, cocoa and coffee supplanted all other cash crops among the Dwabene. The *pɔyɛ* (Twi: *pɔweɛ*; botanical: *Funtumia elastica*) tree that produces latex that is processed into industrial rubber products was native to the land

and grew wildly and abundantly. Tapped latex was either sold to middlemen or directly to merchants in coastal towns in the Gold Coast and Cote d'Ivoire.

The rubber economy created relatively rich men, notable among them Yaw Fum, a recent immigrant from Dadieso and a royal. Yaw Fum was at once young, rich, outgoing, eloquent, cosmopolitan, and brave, and he had grown extremely popular with the pɔyɛfoɛ (rubber latex collectors) and the youth, in general. He was also ambitious and power hungry. It is said that the combination of riches, youth, eloquence, cosmopolitanism, bravery, and, most importantly, his royal pedigree, propelled Yaw Fum to heights where he could easily and quickly organize the pɔyɛfoɛ into a fraternity and political force that would eventually serve his ambition of becoming king of Anyii Dwabene in 1890.

As veritable leader of the pɔyɛfoɛ and king of Anyii Dwabene, Yaw Fum was in an unrivaled powerful position to assert the economic interests of the pɔyɛfoɛ as well as those of Anyii Dwabene, a dual role he played and exploited to the fullest. The new king ruled from Tengualan, a town he had earlier founded and where he was chief prior to ascending the higher Anyii Dwabene stool.

Among Brembi (King) Yaw Fum's collaborators were a few Dwabene chiefs, notable among them Nanou (chief of Manzanouan), Anyimu (chief of Anwaafutu), Boadu (chief of Nyandaa), and Aforo (chief of Dame). Across the frontier in the Gold Coast, Yaw Fum had a strong ally in the person of

Kwadwo Adabo, who is believed to have founded Adabokro (Adabo Town), a bustling Esahié (Sefwi) town on the northern reaches of what is now the Western Region of Ghana, and close to Manzanouan in Anyii Dwabene country in Cote d'Ivoire. Adabo was sometimes called "Osahene," a Twi honorific meaning "chief warrior," an indication of the high respect the people had for his warrior exploits. It is true that Kwado Adabo had participated in a few campaigns in the Gold Coast (the preindependence name of Ghana). In Osahene Adabo, therefore, Nana Yaw Fum could not have found a better ally in his project to challenge and, if possible, oust French colonial influence from Anyii Dwabene.

Together, this loose alliance of likeminded nonconformists aimed to form the bulwark of the resistance to the growing influence of French intruders who, from all indications, were bent on controlling the pɔyɛ or rubber trade, which was the mainstay of Anyii Dwabene economy at the time. In effect, whoever controlled the industry had far-reaching influence on the levers of political power. To Yaw Fum, the mere thought of ceding control of the rubber trade to the French or anybody else was unacceptable, and he was prepared to go to any lengths to prevent that.

Beyond protecting the immediate economic interests of his pɔyɛfoɛ followers, Nana Yaw Fum felt that he had a duty to protect the legitimate economic and political rights of Anyii Dwabene from the encroaching and invasive French colonialists. The

Dwabene had never served under or been controlled by anybody, and he was not going to be the first ruler to place his people under another authority—more so, one they were playing host to. The colonial administration and the state of Dwabene had signed a treaty back in 1892 to, among other things, allow a French trade outpost at Asikaso. To the Anyii, the European guests only wanted a place to set up in order to trade, just as they had welcomed other groups before them. But as the years wore on, it became apparent that the French wanted more than just trade.

King Yaw Fum felt the French not only had him and his Dwabene people in a choking grip, but they were tightening it at the least opportunity. The more he thought about the treaty and the evolving relationship between him and his supposed guests, the more he felt less enthusiastic to keep it. More than once, the proud king of Anyii Dwabene contemplated abrogating the entire agreement, only to back down because he felt the stakes were too high. To his dismay and disappointment, Nana Yaw Fum came to the unpleasant realization that the French had far greater selfish designs on his territory and people than had been thought of at the signing of the Treaty of 1892. He felt his people had been cheated out of their innocence and altruism. He would not allow the situation to continue any further.

By 1897, matters had come to a head, and tempers had become short, frequent, and often feisty, even on issues that hardly drew attention or raised an eyebrow only a few years before. Both sides had grown suspicious of each other on just about anything and everything, and in an atmosphere where there is little trust, the benign oftentimes assume monstrous shapes of mean-spiritedness.

On June 18, 1897, a day to be remembered as a breaking point of the beginning of hostilities between Yaw Fum and the French colonialists, a delegation of administrators had travelled up from the colonial capital on the coast with new decrees they wanted Dwabene indigenes to obey. King Yaw Fum, feeling insulted and belittled, would not oblige and said so in no uncertain terms. He could not fathom the disrespect and audacity of these ungrateful foreign guests who had started to behave as if they owned his kingdom.

Matters did not end there. Yaw Fum went to the French outpost with some of the young men of Dwabene, brandishing guns and other weapons, at the same time warning the few colonial officers guarding the post that he was well-resourced, both in weapons and men, and that he, as host, refused to live by the dictates of a guest. Perhaps the French had set him up or become afraid they might be overrun by Yaw Fum and his forces, who outnumbered them many times over. In any event, the colonial outpost at Asikaso reacted in similar fashion of threat and corky battle readiness. From this point on, it seemed the line had been drawn in the sand, as each side spied the next possible move of the other.

With both sides holding their ground, and in the

absence of any meaningful negotiation to diffuse the tense atmosphere between Yaw Fum's Dwabene loyalists and the few French officials manning the post, it was only a matter of time before something would trigger a confrontation. And as expected and feared, confrontation did occur when Yaw Fum carried out his earlier threat to show that no one walked over him or his kingdom. Early in the morning of April 29, 1898, and without warning, armed young men in battle gear surrounded and laid siege to the French outpost at Asikaso.

Trapped inside and completely outnumbered, all the colonial officers and the few African assistants with them could do and hope for was reinforcement from Bingerville, the colonial capital on the coast. Even though they had superior firepower advantage, commanders at the post reasoned that an offensive would result in large-scale bloodshed on the Dwabene side that would not only win Yaw Fum more followers but would play on the sympathies of neighboring tribes and towns. If that were to happen, then the war would spread beyond Anyii Dwabene and become more difficult to control, with the likely result of a conflagration that could adversely impact the overall colonial project.

For the next sixty-four days (April 29 to July 2, 1898), the French outpost at Asikaso and the perimeter surrounding it became a battleground. As the days wore on, tempers rose higher and higher as both sides grew jittery and more impatient from fatigue and boredom. The number of dead and wounded began to mount, but more on the Dwabene side. Any prospects of negotiations and a peaceful solution grew dangerously dimmer as each day passed.

Yaw Fum's strategy had been to force the surrender of the French by cutting off food, water, and other essential supplies. The strategy was effective initially, because it is reported that the besieged, at some point, resorted to cooking leaves for dinner and squeezing drinking water out of plantain stalks. However, the strategy lasted only so long. The mental fortitude and high morale among the besieged, in the knowledge that help would eventually come from the nearest French garrison or from the main colonial office along the coast, frustrated the Dwabene warriors the more. Also the fact that the Dwabene combatants were no more than a bunch of ragtag young men who were more an angry mob than a disciplined army gave the French officials some hope and the psychological reassurance that they would last longer than the enemy. It would only be a matter of time, they surmised.

From the point of view of Dwabene, it can be argued that the sole objective was to get the French to back down on issuing decrees and playing monarch. In this regard, it can further be argued that the siege was less an act of aggression and more an agitation toward emancipation. Unlike other communities elsewhere during the colonial era, Anyii Dwabene had not signed a treaty seeking protection from the French or anyone, in any shape or form. After all, it was Anyii Dwabene, which a century earlier had rescued and subsequently protected Abron Bonduku from external aggression. So for the French, or any other colonial power for that matter, to take on airs of final authority in Anyii Dwabene, especially with the self-confident Yaw Fum as king, was totally unacceptable.

A breakthrough for the French side finally came when reinforcements arrived from Bingerville in the form of the dreaded and battle-tested battalion of Senegalese sharpshooters popularly known as *tirailleurs sénégalais*. The ferocity of this colonial special forces who later distinguished themselves on the battlefields of Europe and Indochina made all the difference at Asikaso. Though they had stood tall and gallantly for what they believed was in defense of nation and dignity, the Dwabene combatants fell short in the long run, and on July 2, 1898, their resolve buckled, and they fell to superior French firepower and battlefield tactical discipline.

A hasty trial was organized by the victorious French army, and on July 9, 1898, Yaw Fum, king of Anyii Dwabene, along with Nanou (chief of Manzanouan) and Boadu (chief of Nyandaa) were condemned to death and executed by firing squad. The execution of the king and two of his prominent chiefs has, to this day, remained a state oath and a taboo to Anyii Dwabene, so that to invoke Alaka Nza (Twi: Nnakaa Mɛɛnsa; The Three Coffins), in reference to the three coffins that bore the dead bodies of the executed king and two prominent chiefs of Anyii Dwabene, is considered a most serious pronouncement or oath indeed.

Henceforward, French control over Anyii Dwabene would become total and closely guarded, to not leave room for any surprise attack from a people not used to oppression and subjugation. It was also the point in the long history of Anyii Dwabene that the conqueror colonialist prescribed the cultivation of cocoa and later coffee as acceptable economic activity for the indigenes. The French, not market forces, would determine the producer price of cocoa and coffee. In effect, the Dwabene no longer had the right to choose what economic activity to engage in. With a single strike, the colonialists would decide how people should live or prosper. As if all that was not enough, the colonial administration would tax the locals on behalf of the metropolitan government in Paris. The interests of the French overseas possessions became so comprehensive and total the metropolitan administration would not let go without suffering serious economic consequences. To ensure continued control of her overseas territories, the French devised a clever system of sustained colonialism, which they called Departments Outremer, or Overseas Departments.

Awiah Kwaw succeeded Yaw Fum. The new king, reduced in power and authority, had no choice but to go along with French colonial decrees and very often unreasonable demands on his people and the resources of his kingdom. At the same time, the colonial administration kept a close watch over his every utterance, movement, and action. The memory of Asikaso was too fresh to not be on a constant watch over a people still mourning their losses in lives—but more importantly, in pride.

Chapter 6

Migration from Kotokoso

By the end of 1898 and immediately following the failed uprising against French hegemony (the War of Asikaso), which resulted in the execution of Yaw Fum, the eighth king of Anyii Dwabene, and two prominent chiefs, France had finally gained absolute control over the state and citizens of Anyii Dwabene. Among the methods of control, punishment, and subjugation was the inhuman and dreaded forced labor, known in French as *travaux forcés*. This was unremunerated labor required of all able-bodied citizens (mainly men) to build roads and railway lines and perform manual tasks for the colonial administration. Until then, Anyii Dwabene had been spared travaux forcés and similar indignities. In addition to travaux forcés, the French placed inordinate taxes and levies on practically every economic activity Anyii Dwabene citizens engaged in, taxes and levies that did not exist before the War of Asikaso. It was very obvious the French had not finished taking their pound of flesh, so to speak, after the War of Asikaso.

Over time, the draconian French colonial rule created in its wake a quiet revolution, a sort of subdued refusal to obey orders, especially among citizens of Anyii Dwabene whose towns were closer to Ngyeresa (Twi: Inyiresi; British Gold Coast). These analyzed and compared colonial administration as it was practiced by Whitehall, which was less restrictive and more progressive, both in terms of personal freedoms and economic well-being. At a minimum, the British did not practice travaux forcés in the Gold Coast.

Also, British colonialism recognized the important role traditional authority played in the cultural and socioeconomic development of a people. Unlike the French who had overthrown and abolished the rather autocratic and abusive monarchy that had lorded over them some two centuries earlier, the English, on their part, had succeeded in fusing the best from the old and new to fashion out a democratic system comparable to any. As a result, while it was policy with English colonialism to work in partnership with African traditional authority, French colonialism always sought to undermine, weaken, and, if considered safe, even destroy centuries-old African systems of governance.

The benefit to the Anglo-African over his Franco-African counterpart has been the greater awareness and a better appreciation of his culture. The British also found convenient allies in powerful and willing

African traditional rulers to assert control and authority over the natives. The structure of Native Administration, especially as practiced in British West Africa, was premised on working in partnership with a few powerful chiefs and kings or their chosen educated African representatives. The arrangement is sometimes referred to as "indirect rule." Elitist and privileged, indirect rule served the British well because it not only appeased powerful kings who could otherwise challenge colonial authority, the chiefs and kings involved in the system served as a safe buffer between the mass of the people and colonizer.

In French-controlled Anyii Dwabene, accounts of arbitrary arrests and detention on the flimsiest of charges abounded, obviously to drive home the point as to who was in charge. One such narration of the time has it that the colonial governor on the coast sent down a threatening letter written in blood, detailing how he was going to deal with the recalcitrant residents of Kotokoso for failing to carry to the letter one of his many orders. The townspeople had decided the order to pay extra tax unreasonable and even odious, and they had not minced words telling it to the colonial representative of the Canton. And being so close to the border with the Gold Coast where the colonized were freer, the people of Kotokoso could afford to be disrespectful to the French. They knew they had the luxury to slip across the frontier into English territory, the Gold Coast.

Kotokoso had had enough of the dictate and could care less.

Knowing the French for cruelty and perceived unreasonableness, where in place of dialogue or a chance to explain a situation, everything seemed to be "Allez, allez!" (Move on, move on!), the elders of Kotokoso did not want to take chances. Worse, the fact the colonial governor had expressed such bloodcurdling anger in an official communication specifying what was in store for the people of Kotokoso, there was no doubt there would be wholesale humiliation and perhaps casualties. The most senior colonial administrator of the territory was going to set an example with Kotokoso to any who might harbor thoughts of disobeying his orders.

There was no time to speculate or second-guess, or for the opportunity to negotiate with the colonial administration for the mitigation of intended official reprisal, if that was at all possible. Under the circumstance and with time not on their side, the only option left to the residents of Kotokoso was to make a quick exit out of town. Also, the fiasco of resistance that was the War of Asikaso barely twenty years prior, in which the French had executed the king of Dwabene along with two of his senior chiefs, was too fresh on the minds of the people to risk staying put. In short, one of the founding triplets of Anyii Dwabene State, the Kotoko wing, was compelled to depart from the immediate family in order to preserve itself and love of freedom. The immigrants came to their new home more as political refugees than as fugitives because they were not escaping from legitimate law.

In a collaborative piece of work, Adu Boahen and J.B. Webster, two highly respected scholars of African history, seem to corroborate the migratory story of Nkrankwanta as told to me by granduncle Ali Kwadwo Nziah and others:

> In 1900 the French sought to levy a head tax on the entire population and three years later began the construction of a railway which required the seizing of African lands, and increased demands for slave labour. The tax was a total reversal of Afro-French relations as governed by the treaties. Prior to 1900 the French were tribute-paying aliens; by the new tax law they became conquerors exacting a tribute from their former masters.

> … In 1916 the Baulé led another uprising which came almost as close as that of 1908 to expelling the French. In 1917 in hopeless despair of victory the Agni (a people closely related to the Asante) migraed as a body to the less harsh colonialism of the British in neighbouring Ghana.

So they came to live on land that belonged to

a traditional neighbor and that was not their own in Aduana Dormaa. The reigning king of Dormaa is believed to have been Nana Asubonteng, who was Dormaahene by 1911, the same one the Dormaa still fondly remember as "Hene Panin." It is said that Nana was enthroned at a very young age—a boy king, so to speak. Being the king did not prevent him from behaving like the boy that he was, and he was often seen roughing it up in street games with youngsters his age. His handlers at such events would remind the other boys to be careful not to hurt Nana, because he was Hene Panin, the grand chief. Nana Asubonteng's reign broke the silence of a long stretch of rule by regency, during which period Dormaaman had no substantive *omanhene* or king.

The new land may not have been theirs, but the people of Dormaa and Anyii Dwabene were no strangers, one to the other. The two had not only lived as peaceful neighbors since the latter part of the eighteenth century, they had engaged each other and collaborated on many issues and economic fronts, especially in the rubber trade.

As required under Akan tradition, due recognition had to be given to the host or landowner. In other words, one did not enjoy a property or settle on a piece of land without first obtaining the consent and permission of the property owner or landlord. Accordingly, the refugees sought and obtained permission of the omanhene (king) of Dormaa and his traditional council in order to settle on the land. Negotiations between the Anyii Kotoko immigrants and Dormaaman was that the former would pay to the latter a token amount known among the Akan as *asasetoɔ*, which translates as "land use fee" but which is insignificant in value in the real sense of rent. In reality, the asaasetoɔ between Anyii Kotoko and Dormaaman was a symbolic gesture and guarantee that recognized and assured the state of Dormaa of its traditional ownership of land being settled on. By definition and interpretation of that agreement, Nkrankwanta, or Anyii Kotoko, though a significant member of Anyii Dwabene, has no right, traditional or legal, to transfer land from Dormaaman to Anyii Dwabene.

The relationship between the refugee Anyii and their Dormaa hosts was not one of vassalage or as defeated subjects of war, because Anyii Dwabene and Dormaa have never gone to war. Rather, the two ethnic groups have been peaceful and fraternal neighbors, respectful, one of the other. Anyii Dwabene and Dormaa have collaborated on many fronts, going back some two and a half centuries and especially during the period of the rubber trade.

Nana Kwaw Bilé, king of Anyii Dwabene (1934–82)

OSAGYEFO OSEADEYO
DR. AGYEMAN - BADU
(OMANHENE OF DORMAA TRADITIONAL AREA
(1950-1998) AND MEMBER. COUNCIL OF STATE)

Nana Agyeman Badu I, Dormaahene (1950–98). Notice
the Aduana dog totem cast in gold next to him. As
Dormaahene (king of Dormaaman), he is Aduana Piésié,
or head of the Aduana abusua clan of the Akan people.

There is also the compelling evidence that Anyii Dwabene and Dormaa once upon a time lived as neighbors around Amansie, in south-central Ghana. In the respective histories of Anyiii Dwabene and Dormaa, each mentions having left Amansie about the same time—that is, around the end of the eighteenth century. Of particular interest is the fact that the death of Nana Obiri Yeboah, chief of Kumase and uncle to Osei Tutu, the founder of Asanteman or the state of Asante, was a catalyst in the migration stories of the two groups. The evidence of a déjà vu is too strong to overlook or ignore. However, unlike the Dormaa, Anyii Dwabene and Asante never went to war. While the Anyii Dwabene headed southwest from Amansie to Dadieso and finally to Asikaso, the Dormaa, on their part, migrated directly west, establishing towns along the way. For example, the Dormaa had founded and stayed at Bomaa, Kontraagyeso (name later changed to Abesim), Kyeraa, and finally Wam Paamu, which later became Dɔ Wo Man ("Love Your Nation" or "Be a Patriot"). Dɔ Wo Man metamorphosed into Dormaa. The Dormaa had earlier migrated to the Amansie area from Akwamu, in the neighborhood of River Volta, south of the Afram Plains.

In clan or *abusua* relationship in Akandom, Dormaa holds a special position by virtue of the fact she is recognized as Aduana piésié, or "firstborn amongst the Aduana." The Akan people are linked by an extended family system they call abusua. In all, there are eight abusua across the lengths and breadths of the several Akan kingdoms, present and past. The eight abusua are Aduana, Asona, ɛkɔɔna, Bretuo, Agona, Asenie, Asakyiri, and Oyoko. The abusua is a complex system that transcends kingdom and traditional state, to the extent that it is commonplace to find more than one abusua within the boundaries of any given traditional authority. Of the eight abusua, perhaps Aduana is the largest and most ancient.

Anyii Dwabene and Dormaaman also share a common bond and affinity with Abron Bonduku, their older neighbor to the north. For the Anyii, the bond is rooted in the very foundation of Anyii Dwabene State when Abron sought military assistance and protection from Dadieso to get rid of an invading Bouna, her pesky next-door neighbor. The warriors who liberated, and for whose presence in the neighborhood the state of Abron was not to be invaded or threatened again, were rewarded with territory that became the state of Anyii Dwabene. For Dormaaman, the relationship takes in the traditional significance of Nsesreso, a town very close to Bonduku, capital of Abron, from where much of the story of migration and traditional authority finds historical expression. Therefore, Abron Bonduku, as a common point of reference and convergence for both Anyii Dwabene and Dormaaman, is a significant playmaker in relationship and consensus building for her two friendly neighbors to the south.

The Anyii immigrants came with their own stool (the Anyii Kotoko stool), which dates back to the very foundation of Anyii Dwabene, in 1750. They also came with their religious relics and gods, the most famous of which were Nzolε (whose nickname is Akaa Akomea) and the river goddess Soborε, which the Dwabene adopted from the Sefwi.

It is alleged that the Nzolε deity played a significant role in the battle on the plains of Abron in 1750. The story goes that Brédou Assamandje and his soldiers left Dadieso with three things: the blessing of the king and royal court of Dadieso, seven guns with which to do battle, and the spiritual guardianship of Nzolε.

One account of the Bouna-Abron war has it that on reaching the battlefield, the Dwabene warriors invoked Nzolε, thus, "Akaa éé! Akaa Akomea éé!" upon which humanoid gnomes in battle gear appeared from nowhere and in pursuit of enemy Bouna fighters. The Nzolε deity is believed to live in the realm of gnomes, little humanoid beings usually invisible to the naked eye but who can be invoked or summoned to take on form and act as reliable allies and mediums in times of need. This account of the battlefield, though different from the flapping wings of aroused bush fowl, contains the same element of a multitude of objects (frightened birds or released humanoid gnomes) that was key to securing victory for Abron.

Of the original residents of Kotokoso, one elder, Akpo, chose to stay behind with his immediate family. Therefore, the indigenous population of Kotokoso today is largely of the descendants of Kotoko Akpo and the people of Awiasue. Awiasue was a neighbor and smaller Anyii Dwabene community whose residents abandoned their own town and moved en masse to settle the virtually empty space of old Kotokoso. The name of the old town of Anyii Kotoko is still Kotokoso and lies just across the border in Cote d'Ivoire, about six miles from Nkrankwanta.

Notable among the men who led the migration from Kotokoso were Nana Ndri (the chief), Kofi Bilé (he succeeded Ndri as chief), Kofi Amanvo (a.k.a. Kokofioko Kofi), Kwasi Kaa (maternal grandfather of Nana Kwabana Asemia II, Nkrankwantahene), Ndaa Kwabana (junior brother to Kwasi Kaa and maternal great-grandfather to author), Anyimu (later converted to Islam and took the name Isifu), Kwaku Baah (younger brother to Anyimu and maternal grandfather to author; also later converted to Islam and adopted Alhaji as name), Kwabana Asemia (later ascended the throne as Nana Kwabana Asemia), and Kofi Kanga (younger brother to Kwabana Asemia).

Among the women were the following matriarchs: Ekyea Yaa (a.k.a. Yaa Pili; a.k.a. Nana Yaa), believed to have lived to about 120 years; Ekyea Ama (sister to Ekyea Yaa); Buru Akwasi (maternal great-grandmother to author; later converted to Islam and assumed Mariam as name); Akua Tamea (younger sister to Kofi Amamvo); and Ama Soborɛ (later Nana Ama Soborɛ, queen mother). It is important to note that the immigrants from Kotokoso were mostly first and second cousins, one to the other. As a result, marriage between cousins was very common, to the extent that most among the first and second post-migration generations were related by blood on both sides of the family. Naturally, for most first and second generation Anyii Kotoko migrants, inheritance and lineage ran through both sides of the family. The blood ties among members of the earlier small, close-knit community was largely uninterrupted and unbroken.

One must be careful to not show undue bias, but it is appropriate to draw attention to the fact that almost all the male leaders mentioned above, in addition to the matriarchs, except for one (Nana Soborε), were from the Nziah Akpau (Twi: Nsiah Apau) side of the two ruling families of Anyii Kotoko, the other being Ngessah Kwaku (a.k.a. Ngessah Aku) family. I will speak more about the two ruling houses of Nkrankwanta in subsequent pages, but for now, it will suffice to say that not only is Nziah Akpau the larger of the two families, but the first three chiefs—namely Nana Ndri (led Kotoko from Kotokoso and died at New Kotokoso), Nana Kofi Bilé (led Kotoko from New Kotokoso to Old Nkrankwanta), and Nana Kwabana Asemia I (longest occupant of the Kotoko stool to date, who died in 1961)—were all of Nziah Akpau royal family.

In retrospect, the Anyii Dwabene Kotoko stool of Nkrankwanta has been founder of four towns—namely Kotokoso, New Kotokoso, Old Nkrankwanta, and Nkrankwanta. Of the four, Kotokoso and Nkrankwanta are still inhabited. Kotokoso (Fr. Kotokosso) is located in Cote d'Ivoire while Nkrankwanta is in Ghana. The distance between the two towns is about six miles. In short, the history of the Kotoko stool did not begin at Nkrankwanta.

Chapter 7

The Founding of Nkrankwanta

Big Little River

By the river,
Yes, by the Big River!
A carpet below the valley
In a crescent formation,
On the edges of town,
Width wide enough to challenge a triple-jumper
But a source of protection and succor
To the people who believed and worshipped.

Drink but eat not
Its fruits-de-mer.
Tales of angry pythons if violated.
Madness, even death
The consequences of
Fluvial insubordination.
Pacification resets the equilibrium.

Like the Soborε of old,
Le Grand Fleuve of sustenance and fecundity
Loomed large in the hearts
Of the founding pioneers.

And they believed in
Her majestic humility.
So let her be,

Nzué Pili, the little Big River.

Name Origin

Ngala Ngwandaa (Nkra Nkwanta) loosely translates as "the Crossroads of Farewell." The name originated from the fact the town is situated at the crossroads of the old trade routes.

In the olden days when people used to travel on foot to distant commercial centers like Oguaa (Cape Coast), Sekune (Sekondi), Takyima (Techiman), Wankyi (Wenchi), Kumase, or Yaane (Yendi), this crossroads was where people from nearby towns and villages would bid farewell, between travelers and those seeing them off. The paths leading to these far-off commercial centers all converged at this Ngwandaa or Nkwanta (junction or crossroads). At the time, the people of Anyii Kotoko who founded Ngala Ngwandaa or Nkrankwanta had their home at Kotokoso (Kotoko-So), a town some six miles across the border in present-day Cote d'Ivoire, which still bears the same name. When Anyii Kotoko had to permanently relocate, it was easy and most convenient to set camp at or in the neighborhood of a spot that was so well known to them. They named the place Ngala-Ngwandaa, meaning Crossroads of Farewell. Nkra-Nkwanta, and for that matter Nkrankwanta, the officially recognized name of this Anyii Dwabene town, is the Twi rendition of Ngala-Ngwandaa.

The founding and evolution of Nkrankwanta is as daring, interesting, and dramatic as the history behind why a people well-ensconced on their own land and living among their own kind were compelled to start life all over again in someone else's territory and in a new environment, however friendly and welcoming their new home. But the relative safety and freedom under the Ngyeresa (Nyiresi or English) British Gold Coast compared to their experiences under French colonialism were worth the dislocation, pain, and uncertainties of migration. The migration was in three stages and took approximately sixteen years to complete, culminating in the present location of Nkrankwanta in 1917.

From Kotokoso in Cote d'Ivoire, the emigrants crossed the colonial frontier and settled at a location about one mile inside Gold Coast territory. I will call this first settlement New Kotokoso, though it is now referred to as Amamvoso (Twi: Amamfoso) or Old Fort. The year was 1900 or 1901. New Kotokoso was within earshot of old Kotokoso in French territory, a mere two-mile distance between the two towns.

The emigrants intended New Kotokoso as a temporary resting place, hoping the threat from the French colonial governor to severely punish them and perhaps sack their town would dissipate well enough so they could return to their old homes at Kotokoso. They hoped that the colonial administration might relax in the desire to punish them for alleged insubordination, stemming from the refusal to obey orders the Anyii considered too harsh and unreasonable. But after a lengthy wait with information still suggesting severe punishment would be meted out to them if they returned, the emigrants resigned themselves to fate and instead focused on making the best of the situation—that is, to move on. The stay at New Kotokoso is estimated to have lasted about eleven years.

The group headed further east and settled by a stream almost opposite where the Nkrankwanta Secondary Technical High School is located, on the main Nkrankwanta–Krakrom road. I will refer to this place as Old Nkrankwanta. The stay at Old Nkrankwanta lasted about six years, because floodwaters from the river during the rainy seasons forced the emigrants to once again relocate, to about one mile uphill. There is consensus that the final leg of the migration and founding of Nkrankwanta occurred in 1917.

The new settlement was close to Nzué Pili (Twi: Asu Kɛseɛ) or Big River, whose size and flow does not reflect its name. Perhaps the bigness of Nzué Pili is in the fact it is bigger than the other river on the peripheries of town, the river along which Old Nkrankwanta was founded. Equally significant is the fact the settlers deferred to Nzué Pili the religious status of the river god Soborɛ, which was introduced earlier in this book as the river god of fertility the migrating Anyii Dwabene had borrowed from, and shared with, the Esahié (Sefwi) on the maiden migration from Amansie to Dadieso. Aside from drinking from its waters, no other resource is consumed from Nzué Pili because of the religious attachment the founding pioneers ascribed to it.

The environment the first settlers met was unfriendly; after all, it was uninhabited territory. For the next few decades, the immigrants shared space with wild animals. Leopards were a common sight because these forest big cats preyed on livestock, especially sheep and goats from the pens of the townsfolk. And in order to protect their livestock, the brave among the residents, working in teams, would hunt down these ferocious carnivores with guns and machetes. Bravery in those days, especially in self-defense and in the face of extreme danger, defined a man. But one has to be fair to the wildlife because, in truth, it was the immigrants who had encroached and squatted on their territory and not the other way around.

Almost every community or people have some legend associated with their origins or collective experiences. A piece of the history of Nkrankwanta, specifically as regards its phenomenal growth from a relatively insignificant settlement less than a century ago, revolves around a *sumi* or magical talisman that is said to have been buried on the fringes of town. "Insignificant" because any map sixty years or older seldom mentioned Nkrankwanta (Akrakwato, as later maps called the town), whereas neighboring Krakrom and Diabaakrom have received front-page recognition from just about any cartographer who mapped this midwest corner of the then Gold Coast. Nkrankwanta was simply too small to merit a spot on the cartographer's drawings and charts.

The story of the magical talisman, which has been told and retold by just about every elder familiar with the story of Nkrankwanta's rapid and phenomenal growth, is that the pioneers consulted with one Serekye Hejira (El Hajj Sadiq), a very learned and spiritually developed Islamic man in the town of Yorobodi, in Anyii Barebo country, for spiritual assistance in order that their new settlement would grow into an important town. The narration continues that the spiritual man, after several weeks of fasting and intense prayers, produced a talisman with instructions to bury it as far out as the visiting elders of Nkrankwanta would want their town to expand to. The elders did as they were instructed and buried their cherished talisman so far away that many among them doubted their little town would ever stretch out that far.

Those who claim to know where the talisman that was inspired and created in Barebo was buried can swear that the town has outstripped many times the location of the Sumi of Nkrankwanta. This is an interesting historical account—one example of shared experience among peoples the world over yet an experience that does not lend itself to scientific or logical scrutiny. The story of the Sumi of Nkrankwanta rests in the realm of belief and blind faith, in the world of metaphysics where believers will vouch evidence yet cannot provide concrete proof to substantiate the alleged evidence. But is human experience, or the nature of things, restricted to or founded only on what the senses can feel and touch?

Back to those who believe the expansionist talisman of Nkrankwanta has played a central role in the town's success story. Any narration or commentary about the history of their town would be incomplete until the Sumi of Nkrankwanta has been accorded due recognition and a place in the town's interesting history.

Neighbors and Good Samaritans

Beside Dormaa Ahenkro (Royal Capital of the Dormaa), other towns had already been settled by the time the Anyii Dwabene from Kotokoso founded Nkrankwanta. Among these were Kokorasua, Yaakro, Nsuhia, and Asikasu. In the immediate vicinity were Diabaakrom and Krakrom. It is estimated that Krakrom had been settled some forty years earlier. Indeed, it was through the friendship and altruism of these first neighbors, especially Diabaakrom and Krakrom, that the new settlers obtained foodstuffs like plantains and cocoyams for their immediate needs. It is also from these already settled communities that the new immigrants obtained seedlings to plant their own food crops.

The elders make special mention of Nana Yaw Diabaa, founder of Diabaakrom, who not only persuaded Anyii Kotoko to relocate further inland but also spoke well of the environment and life support opportunities. For the immigrants, emotional attachment to their old town across the frontier, coupled with lingering thoughts that a time would come for them to return to old Kotokoso, weighed heavily on their minds. But the friendship and good neighborliness of the earlier settlers cushioned the nostalgia about old Kotokoso. As proof of good neighborliness, Nana Yaw Diabaa adopted one of my granduncles, Kwadwo Nziah, who later converted to Islam and took the Muslim name Ali. Much of this book has been the narration Ali Kwadwo Nziah passed on to me since from when I was a little boy and over a period of some thirty years. Kofi Tawiah, another granduncle and a younger brother to Kwadwo Nziah, was also adopted by one Opanin Kyereh at Dormaa Ahenkro. The adoptions were not as a result of parental irresponsibility or abandonment of these young men; they were the manifestation of great friendship. In much of Africa, one sometimes adopts to cement family ties or as a show of deep friendship to the adoptee parents or extended family. The gesture is in the expression: "I will raise your child as if he was my own."

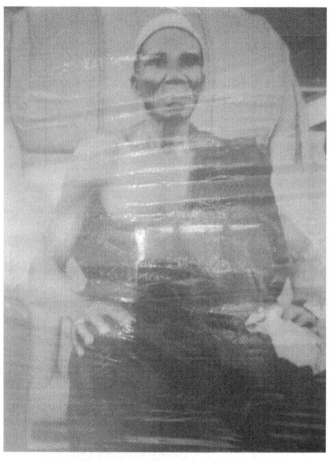

Ali Kwadwo Nziah. A walking encyclopedia of Dwabene history and customs, he bequeathed through the oral tradition method a very significant amount of information that went into this book.

However, the early experiences of the immigrants were not all friendly or as beneficiaries of others' altruism. The story is told, and retold, of a few lazy and opportunistic Dormaa indigenes who took pleasure at intimidating and duping the new settlers, whom they found quite vulnerable. These miscreants would purport to be bearing instructions from the Dormaahene (king of Dormaa) to collect money or some other valuables. The do-nothings and societal parasites would precede their statement of extortion with, "Nana dɛ ..." (Nana, or the king, says ...), followed by the demand for one specific valuable or other. In addition, there were those who would harvest from farms cultivated by the Anyii immigrants and rationalize the theft as taking from land belonging to Nana and the people of Dormaa, oblivious to the fact that the owner had worked hard to transform a forest of trees into a farm of crops.

The practice went on for some time, until the residents of Nkrankwanta developed a collective sixth sense and suspected the whole thing was a scheme by the lazy and irresponsible in society to feed on their sweat and hard work. The immigrants further suspected that these Dormaa indigenes were out to take advantage of their relative vulnerability as newcomers from a different traditional authority and culture. But first the elders sent messengers to enquire from Nana Dormaahene if the many and revolving door "Nana dɛ ..." were true palace emissaries sent to collect *asasetoɔ*, the token annual land-use fee the new immigrants had negotiated with the landowner Dormaahene. When it was established that the "Nana dɛ ..." were rather layabouts and parasites and had no direct link to the king, nor had they been instructed to collect any dues, the elders devised a plan of action to deal with the miscreants.

The next time someone came with a "Nana dɛ ..." request or demand, and before he could finish his statement of lies, one or other of the elders would instruct the nearest young men in Anyii thus: "am ɔ bo ye!" ("Beat the crap out of him!"). This rather vigilante solution worked so well that in no time, the extortionist "Nana dɛ ..." ways of the lazy and do-nothing was defeated, placed in a coffin, firmly nailed down, and finally entombed.

Chapter 8

Anyii Kotoko Stool

Nkrankwanta lays claim to the Kotoko title because she is the Oyoko wing of Anyii Dwabene. This unit of Dwabene state is so conscious of its abusua affiliation that it named its maiden town Kotoko-So. The town still stands as Kotokoso, just across the frontier in Cote d'Ivoire, but is now home to a smaller neighbor community that moved in after most of the Kotoko people had deserted to found Nkrankwanta. Kotoko is one-third of Anyii Dwabene by virtue of it being one of three original stools of Anyii Dwabene state. The others are Agniblékro and Dame. However, Agniblékro retains the paramountcy.

The relationship is so deep that when the chief (*famea* in Anyii) or other high-ranking royal passes on at Nkrankwanta, custom dictates that the chief of Dame has exclusive right to announce the sad news, including decisions on burial and other rites of passage. In other words, there is none but the chief of Dame who has the traditional authority to announce the death of the Kotokohene or chief of Nkrankwanta or any other high-ranking Kotoko royal, or perform funeral and other rites. The custom is reciprocal when a similar sad event occurs at Dame. For, after all, the two stools were carved from the same piece of wood, one after the other, in 1750.

Custom further dictates that the chiefs of Nkrankwanta, Dame, and Ngesakro together exercise exclusive right to announce the passing of an Anyii Dwabene Brembi or king. The three towns also manage burial arrangements. It is Anyii Dwabene custom, pure and simple. Any other way would be out of the woods and a sacrilege to Anyii Dwabene custom and usage. It is what it is.

I have mentioned above that Anyii Kotoko is of the Oyoko clan. This fact is evident on palace *hɔtɔ* (golden staff of authority) bearing the falcon, which is totem for Ayoko (plural of Oyoko) stools everywhere among the Akan. The Oyoko is one of eight clans or family units (abusua) that every Akan must belong to. The eight Akan Abusua, in random order, are as follows:

	Abusua Name	Akyenaboa (Insignia or Totem)
1.	Aduana (a.k.a. Atwea, Abrade, Amoakare ne Ada)	Dog
2.	Asona	Crow
3,	ɛkoɔna (a.k.a. Kwɔnnafo, ɛkoɔ ne Asimpi. Ahweniɛ a ɛda yaawa mu, Asɔ kɔrefoɔ)	Buffalo

4.	Bretuo ne Tena (Fantse—Twidanfo)	Leopard
5.	Agona (Fantse—Eguanafo)	Parrot
6.	Asenie (Fantse—Atwafo)	Bat
7.	Asakyiri (a.k.a. Amoakaadefɔ. Fantse—Anonafo)	Hawk
8.	ɔyɔko (Yɔkofo or Dehyena in Fantse). ɔyɔko is often spelt "Oyoko", the same way Kɔtɔkɔ is written "Kotoko"	Falcon

Further evidence of Nkrankwanta's Oyoko heritage is the fact they named their original home Kotoko-So. Also when the *atumbgala* (Twi: *atumpan*) talking drums summon the indigenes of Nkrankwanta to assemble over a grave or critical matter, they intone in Asante Twi: "Kotoko mo mra! Kotoko mo mra! Kotoko mo mra! Mo mra! Mo mra! Mo mra!" (People of Kotoko assemble! People of Kotoko assemble! People of Kotoko assemble! Assemble! Assemble! Assemble!).

I developed a profound interest in the history of Anyii Dwabene, and especially of Nkrankwanta, at a very tender age. Perhaps also, coming from the Nzia Akpau royal lineage and being the oldest of my siblings, clan elders had put in place an elaborate plan to gradually pass on the oral history of my people, as has been handed down to succeeding generations over time. I would be invited to listen in to discussions at meetings of family and clan elders, which events were the perfect settings to hear and learn about important happenings and stories of the past. At such meetings, one also gets to learn and understand a great deal about the people's collective experience and worldview, often couched in proverbs or short statements of fact. Later in life and even as I sojourned away from home to eventually live in North America, I continued to receive doses of historical happenings recorded on electronic cassette tapes. Much of this work, therefore, is the retelling of what I have been told since from about the age of ten. In other words, I am passing on the oral history of Anyii Kotoko (and related topics) but in the print form and to a wider audience.

There is one very interesting historical account I want to retell. A great-granduncle went to Kumase in the days when travel was by foot and through dense forests. Unbeknownst to this great-granduncle, an important Asante royal, perhaps the king himself, had died. As was the practice in those days everywhere among the Akan, some rituals had to be performed before announcement was made of such a great loss. Among the rituals was human sacrifice.

During one of his walkabouts in Kumase, my great-granduncle was accosted and detained by *abrafo* (royal executioners). It was also the practice, or must I say the protocol, for royal executioners to ascertain from a captive his origins, lest they shed the blood of the wrong person. The narration continued that when my great-granduncle mentioned he was an Anyii Kotoko royal, he was let go, meaning he was not one for ritual sacrifice. Perhaps there was some password, confidential code, or a specific answer to some question known only to someone from a particular home or lineage, as was often the case in times of war or national emergency, that my ascendant was able to answer correctly and, as a result, save his neck from the executioner's knife.

In times gone by, it was not uncommon for someone to travel to any place in Akandom and be hosted by hitherto total strangers on account of belonging to the same abusua. In other words, an Aduana, Asona, or a Bretuo could travel to any of the several Akan kingdoms, and once his hosts were convinced he was of the same larger abusua, family or clan, the stranger would be hosted as if he were a local blood relative. It is obvious there must have been a way of identifying members of the same abusua, as in for example a secret code, a specific way of greeting and response, one's hometown and specific information on immediate family, or the knowledge of a piece of history that is kept within the circles of the clan. In the case of the narration about my great-granduncle, it is very likely the executioners decided to spare his life because, like the royals who sit on the throne of Asante, he was able to prove he was from the same Oyoko abusua.

The Two Ruling Houses of Nkrankwanta

Two founding houses are legitimate inheritors of Anyii Kotoko stool and between them elect chiefs and queen mothers. None from outside these two families qualify to sit on the Kotoko stool. They are Nziah Akpau (Nsiah Apau) and Ngessah Kwaku (a.k.a. Ngessah Aku) families. These two were brothers and of Anyii Dwabene stock. To emphasize, and for the avoidance of doubt, any claimant to Anyii Kotoko throne not matrilineally a direct descendant of Nziah Akpau or Ngesah Kwaku is, without a doubt, a pretender and a usurper. Following are past Anyii Kotoko chiefs dating from the migration from Kotokoso:

	Name	Length of Rule*	Ruling House	Comments
1.	N'dri	1895–1906	Nziah Akpau	Last chief of Anyi Kotoko at Kotokoso. Led the emigrants across the border to New Kotokoso in Ngyeresa (Inyiresi) Gold Coast territory. He died and was buried at New Kotokoso. His remains were later exhumed and reburied at present-day Nkrankwanta.
2.	Kofi Bilé	1906–1921	Nziah Akpau	Was enthroned at New Kotokoso. Led his people further inland, to Old Nkrankwanta. Location was by the river on Nkrankwanta-Krakrom road and almost opposite Secondary Technical High School. Recurring flooding forced another migration. In 1917, the migrants relocated uphill, built and formed a nucleus around their palace.

3.	Kwabana Asemia I	1921–1961	Nziah Akpau	Died in 1961.
4.	Kofi Asemia (a.k.a. Kofi Kra)	1961–1967	Ngessah Kwaku	First time.
5.	Kwame Agyei	1967–1968	Ngessah Kwaku	Abdicated because of an unexplained illness that affected his vocal chords. He was barely audible when he spoke.
6.	Kofi Asemia (a.k.a. Kofi Kra)	1968–1978	Ngessah Kwaku	Second time. Nana Kofi Asemia was an absentee chief much of his tenureship. He lived in Abidjan and seldom visited Nkrankwanta or communicated with the elders at home. Nkrankwanta was effectively under regency.
7.	Kwabana Asemia II	1978 – 2015	Ngessah Kwaku	Died April 23, 2015, shortly before the publication of this book.

Note: some dates are close approximations.

81

Nana Kwabana Asemia I seated with some of his elders. His long and wise rule continues to influence the affairs of the Kotoko stool of Nkrankwanta.

It is evident from the above list that the stool name Asemia has dominated since from the final migration and founding of New Nkrankwanta. Though Kwabana Asemia I (the longest-serving chief to date) was of Nziah Akpau lineage, the stool name he bore has been preferred by subsequent Ngessah Aku stool occupants. This fact underscores the common bond and shared heritage of the two ruling families, until recent unfortunate events. But Anyii Kotoko will reorganize and prevail in unity as before, because the agents of division are not of royalty whose taunts and actions, though an aberration, will last only for as long as they are tolerated. Similarly, any designs to rewrite the history of Anyii Kotoko and hence of Nkrankwanta will be null and void. For the simple reason that a revisionist history of Kotoko will not fit in with the broader setup of Anyii Dwabene as in, for example, the special roles played by Nkrankwanta, Dame, and Ngesakro in times of national emergency. A revisionist idea will be dead on arrival.

There is a constant in human affairs, and it is this: it may be possible to reorder or even change the present, but it is impossible to permanently reorder or change a people's past or collective experience, which is the same as saying that we can tinker with the present but not with true history. More so, when that experience or history is etched in the complexities of the spoken word, talking drums, age-old customs and traditions, and in other cultural artifacts unique to a people, the attempt to falsify may succeed but temporarily. The history of Anyii Kotoko, or Nkrankwanta, may be tinkered with, but the truth about the past will not allow itself to be doctored or changed. It is so ingrained in Dwabene culture that any attempt at a permanent falsification of history, customary practices, and conventions will be easily exposed; the joints will simply not fit or match.

Political Organization at Nkrankwanta

Although the founders of Nkrankwanta were of the Anyii Dwabene stock, they were joined a few decades later by immigrants from other Anyii subgroups, notably Mɔrɔfo, Indenie, Bini, and Abɛɛ. To the uninitiated and untrained eye, Nkrankwanta consists of one monolithic Anyii group that speaks the Dwabene variety of Anyii. But there are subtleties. I must quickly point out that intermarriage among the different Anyii subgroups has, to a large degree, obscured much of those subtleties and distinct family lines. For some time now, whenever I visit home after a considerably long stay abroad, an elder from my Anyii Dwabene side will lead me to heads of each of the four other Anyii subgroups to express condolences as well as make funeral donations regarding members who passed away since my last visit. This is whether or not my family made donations on my behalf at the actual funeral during my absence. The gesture is to emphasize the strong relationship among all the Anyii groups at Nkrankwanta.

While the Anyii Dwabene migration was as a direct result of persecution at the hands of the French colonialists, that was hardly the case for the other Anyii groups. In the case of the Mɔrɔfo, Indenie, Bini, Abɛɛ, and later a few other Akan groups from Cote d'Ivoire who came to settle at Nkrankwanta, it was more economic migration than anything else, since at the time the Gold Coast had a relatively better developed economy than Cote d'Ivoire. One popular "Sida" song that did the rounds beautifully captured the mood of the times this way:

Ghana éé! éé! ... bɛ lɛ sikaa a, bɛngɔ Ghana
Ghana éé!, atomoli, bɛ lɛ sikaa a, bɛngɔ Ghana

Translation:
One needs a deep pocket to enjoy a trip to Ghana.
My darling, one needs a deep pocket to enjoy a trip to Ghana.

A distinguishing feature of the migration between the first settlers—namely the Dwabene and the other Anyii groups (Mɔrɔfo, Bini, Abɛɛ, Indenie, etc.)—is that whereas the former came with a stool, the rest came without, a clear indication that, properly speaking, their roots, or stool allegiance, lay or continued to lie elsewhere. This also means that primary qualification to the Kotoko stool, or the privilege of playing a kingmaker role, is determined, first and foremost, by matrilineal linkage to Anyii Dwabene. Therefore, to be legitimate, an occupant of the Anyii Kotoko stool must be a direct descendant of one of the two founding Anyii Dwabene houses, which is the same as saying that qualification and eligibility for stool candidacy cannot be other than by direct descendancy of either Nzia Akpau or Ngesah Kwaku (Ngesah Aku). However, this arrangement does not preclude or prevent non-Dwabene Anyii, or other longtime resident groups for that matter, from holding important advisory positions or from playing decision-making roles in the court of traditional administration. In fact, representatives from each of the non-Dwabene Anyii have sat in council since the founding of Nkrankwanta.

The candidate nomination process is a laborious task that may take a few days or extend into weeks and even months, depending on prevailing circumstances. Several qualified candidates from either the Nzia Akpau or Ngessah Aku line of succession may be placed on a preliminary list. Having considered all qualified and eligible candidates, the list is pared down to two or three individuals. It is from this shortlist that the kingmakers will inform the elders and queen mother of a new chief. The kingmakers are themselves made up of elders from the Nziah Akpau and Ngesah Kwaku royal houses. However, the kingmakers may include carefully selected elders from any of the other Anyii groups, namely Mɔrɔfo, Indenie, Bini, and Abɛɛ.

To be eligible for candidate selection, a potential occupant of Anyii Kotoko stool must have two basic qualities: he must be of good character and must be of sound physical disposition. In other words, to be considered for the role of chief, a candidate must have given sufficient proof and assurance he will not bring shame and ridicule to the stool. It is also expected of him that as leader of the community, he will instill unity, confidence, respect, uprightness in character, and good behavior among his subjects and beyond.

By good character is meant the future chief must command respect among his peers and must be generally liked. He must be law abiding and considered wise by all who have been in his company. For example, an individual with a criminal record or known not to be of sound mind will not be eligible for the position of chief of Anyii Kotoko. So will one who has alienated himself from his extended family and community, because, in essence, a chief or king among the Anyii Dwabene and indeed among all Akan groups must be available and approachable. Therefore, one considered detached from the community cannot truly serve that community. Other soft or nonphysical qualities are expected of a candidate to Anyii Kotoko stool, but uppermost among them is that the future chief must be at home with Dwabene custom and usage, least among them a mastery of the Anyii Dwabene language.

In sum, good character means moral uprightness as defined by the norms of Anyii Dwabena and the prevailing worldview of the immediate larger society. As to what constitute morality and virtue, though the definition may change in place and time even within the same community, the determining factor is the collective acceptance of behaviors and values.

As is true of every community or people the world over, the Anyii Dwabene worldview is shaped by the sum total of the people's collective experience and shared history. It is equally true to say that among all communities and peoples the world over, exogenous pressure on collective experience, if unchecked, has the potential or tendency to distort and even unhinge a community from its foundation and moorings. Notwithstanding, there are common and shared universal values, based on truth. These are because they are universally accepted and ungrudgingly so.

To be considered of sound physical disposition, the future chief or king must be whole in body. This means that he must not have any debilitating physical condition. For example, he must have full use of his eyes, ears, hands, legs, and voice. He must not have lost any of his fingers or toes or be deformed in any other part of the body. In the olden days, and before many royals among the Akan converted to Islam or Christianity, circumcision was considered a deformity, for the reason that a significant chunk of the male organ had been lobbed off, leaving a stunted and therefore incomplete manhood. Many non-Akan have found this aspect of ancient Akan culture a source of subdued mirth and stereotypical entertainment. Circumcision is no longer a deformity in the selection process of a chief or king among the Akan.

Female elders from Nziah Akpau and Ngesah Kwaku royal houses play advisory roles in candidate eligibility and qualification decisions. Their advice is almost always taken. The chosen candidate is presented to the queen mother and female elders of both Nziah Akpau and Ngesah Aku for confirmation. If for whatever reason the queen mother wants to reject the nominee after the long selection process, then she must give reasons acceptable to the female elders and male kingmakers of both Nziah Akpau and Ngesah Aku families gathered. In other words, unlike among Akan Twi-Fante, a queen mother in Anyii Dwabene does not have the equivalent of veto power. The queen mother's decision in the candidate selection process can be ignored if the elders find her unreasonable. As a result, the queen mother among the Anyii does not, and cannot, block a popular choice of the elders or unilaterally appoint a new chief. It is Anyii custom and usage.

It is obvious throughout this discussion that among Anyii Dwabene, no one person, regardless of station or status, has the prerogative or authority to *enstool*, and for that matter *destool*, a chief or queen mother. Enstoolment or destoolment is a closely guarded collective process that is managed by a council of elders or kingmakers. It is a democratic process that is held in awe and strictly guarded. Where that principle has been violated, the chief or queen mother so crowned would command no more than feigned allegiance and support of the people because his or her legitimacy would have been compromised.

Immediately after he has been announced as the preferred choice from the list of eligible candidates, a mock display of assault and humiliation on the person of the confirmed candidate takes place. Young men "beat up" the new chief by hitting him lightly. The "assault" symbolizes a last act of peer relationship with a soon-to-be elevated ordinary son of the people who may not be insulted, roughed up, or hit after his enstoolment. The young men also tear off the clothes he wore to the coronation grounds, signifying his transition from an ordinary life to a higher station, where he will soon be changing into clothes and sandals that have been worn by his ancestors, some dating back a century or more.

Early on the day of his coronation, the new chief is seated on the ancient Bia Bilé black stool that represents the collective soul of his people. The seating on the stool is preceded by the pouring of libation to God Almighty and the ancestors—for long life, prosperity, and protection from evil. In the case of Nkrankwanta, it is the stool that was carved from the same piece of wood along with those of AnyiniBilékro and Dame in 1750. Also it is the same stool Nana Ekyea Yaa (a.k.a. Yaa Pili, a.k.a. Nana Yaa) bore on her head during the epic migration from Kotokoso of old. Nana will sit on the ancient stool very briefly, perhaps made to touch it with his buttocks three times, because custom forbids a chief to sit on the Bia Bilé for an extended period of time. It is believed among Anyii Dwabene that a longer than reasonable seating on the ancient stool could render the chief incapable of having any more children. This act of the installation process takes place away from the public eye.

Immediately following the seating ceremony, the new chief is ushered into the palace grounds to swear to his people. Holding firm in his right hand the state sword of authority, cloth slightly lowered down the shoulder, and feet slightly removed from his sandals in a show of humility and respect to the people and their stool, the new chief commits to lead and defend his people, the Anyii Kotoko, their heritage, dreams, and aspirations, and to withhold the good name and spirit enshrined in the Anyii Kotoko stool. The cloth in this context is the traditional outwear of the Akan people, which consists of one piece of rich cotton material that is thrown over the upper body and gathered on the left shoulder, leaving the upper right chest and shoulder visible and free. One or two young men hold the new chief gently by the waist to give support as he swears the oath of office. Soon after, the talking drums bellow appellations, with the palace horn blowers filling the air with sounds from horns from elephant tusks.

The new chief is introduced to the gathered crowd, who is told the stool name of their new stool occupant, a name that will most likely be different from the one he was known by immediately before his coronation. Henceforward, he is addressed as "Nana," the honorific reserved for kings, chiefs, and queen mothers. The new Nana is smeared with talcum powder or white ochre to symbolize victory, his victory and that of his people. He is carried shoulder high or in a palanquin borne on the heads of a few strong young men and paraded through a section of town or at least, around the forecourt of the palace where the swearing in and other ceremonies had earlier taken place. Womenfolk from his immediate family dress in white and smear themselves with white ochre or talcum powder.

It is important to make this point about the sacred stool among the Anyii and all other Akan tribes or groups: one who carries the stool does not sit on it. Therefore, though Nana Yaa (a Nzia Akpau) was of royal lineage and eminently qualified, the fact she carried the Kotoko stool from Kotokoso to Nkrankwanta excluded her from consideration for the position of queen mother.

Nana Yaa Pili truly lived by her nickname. Pili (Twi: Kɛseɛ) means muscular, big, or strong. Not that Ekyea Yaa was overly big in size, but there is no denying the fact that she was physically strong. Several eyewitness accounts relate how she used to haul two hundred plantain suckers from Diabaakrom (carrying one hundred, with another one hundred tied to her back) and walk the six-mile distance to the newly settled Nkrankwanta. This was during the first year after migration to Old Nkrankwanta, when the new arrivals needed crop seedlings from neighboring Diabaakrom and Krakrom to cultivate their own food crops.

It is therefore no surprise the consensus among narrators that Ekyea Yaa (a.k.a. Yaa Pili, a.k.a. Nana Yaa) bore the Anyii Kotoko stool on her head from

New Kotokoso to Old Nkrankwanta, a distance of some six miles. As mentioned, the one who carries the stool does not sit on it, and for this reason, even though she had all the royal qualifications to have been elected queen mother of Nkrankwanta, Nana Yaa was passed over for Nana Soborε. Perhaps also the kingmakers decided to not have Nziah Akpau keep both the chief-ship and queen-mother-ship. Nana Yaa was a Nziah Akpau while Nana Soborε was a Nguessah Aku. Another evidence Nana Yaa carried the Kotoko stool from Kotokoso to Nkrankwanta is the fact that her male descendants have the traditional role of stool custodians.

It is important to mention that in spite of its relatively small size, the Bia Bilé or sacred stool is no ordinary stool. It is believed to contain the soul and spirit of the people since from time immemorial, and to have spiritual forces inhabiting it. Therefore, there are moments when the stool being carried between two points will hesitate, rest, accelerate, or simply get so heavy, some porters look like they have rubber for feet as they sweat in beads. It is a well-known fact that traditionally designated stool carriers (*biasoafoε* in Anyii; *nkonwasoafo* in Twi) are often seen sweating under the weight of the otherwise "small" and "light" stools they bear on their heads, even over very short distances. This fact is further evidence in support of narrations that it was the strong Ekyea Yaa who carried the Kotoko stool on the maiden journey from Kotokoso.

By strict Akan usage, every major stool has

dedicated caretakers who constitute an arm of the administrative structure and hierarchy of palace government. The Biasoafoε in Anyii, and Nkonwasoafoɔ in Twi, are the traditional custodians of the royal stool who perform the necessary temporal and spiritual duties required of their office. In Ghana, where Akan culture is older and therefore more developed than in Cote d'Ivoire, the office of stool caretaker is under the leadership of a subchief variously called Nkonwasoafohene, Nsafoahene, or Dabehene.

In coming days, weeks, and perhaps months, the new chief will undergo some customary training and spiritual development sessions in the secrecy of a section within the palace gates or at a secret location out of town. The curriculum for the customary training will be drawn up and administered by the elders, male and female. Foremost on the list of subjects will be the do's and dont's of his new station as chief. Nana will be taught the history of his people. He will also be taught general chiefly protocol. For example, henceforward, he will not quarrel, fight, or hit anyone with his hand; he will not eat or drink at public gatherings; and he will avoid falling into bad company in order to safeguard his personal image as chief and, by extension, the image of the Anyii Kotoko stool. Among the Akan, a chief or king is not his person; he is the embodiment of his people and ancestors. In other words, a chief or king among the Akan is an extension of the stool he sits on, or he represents the collective will and aspirations of all who owe allegiance to that stool.

Custom dictates that a new chief swear allegiance to the people of Nkrankwanta. Shortly after, the new Nkrankwantahene introduces himself to Nana Dormaahene (king of Dormaaman) or his representative and Dwabenefamea (king of Anyii Dwabene). The introduction of a new chief to the Dormaahene (or his assign) and Dwabenefamea is not required to follow any particular order. The convention over the years has been to first introduce Nana Nkrankwantahene to Nana Dormaahene (or his assign), perhaps for two reasons: (1) he is closer in Ghana than the Dwabenefamea, who resides at AnyiniBilékro, across the frontier in Cote d'Ivoire; and (2) it is appropriate to first introduce himself to the landlord as the new tenant chief on his land. In the early years, the chief of Asikasu was Nana Dormaahene's designated liaison in relations with Nkrankwanta. But a recent rearrangement has the chief of Amasu, who doubles as Ankobeahene of Dormaa Traditional Area, as middleman.

I must quickly note that the introduction process is a matter of courtesy only. The fact AnyiniBilékro and Nkrankwanta, from among the entire Anyii Dwabene state, observe their respective yam festivals on the same day is indicative of the notion of primus inter pares (first among equals) between the two senior sibling towns. It is also important to note that with the exception of colonial authority, Anyii Dwabene has never been defeated in war, nor served under any traditional authority. Rather, it is Anyii Dwabene, and by extension Nkrankwanta, that has been sought after to liberate and protect kingdoms in distress, as was the case with the ancient and powerful kingdom of Abron Bonduku. And by virtue of the fact the occupant of the Kotoko stool at Nkrankwanta is effectively the Kotoko Famea (Kotokohene, chief of the Kotoko wing) of Anyii Dwabene, to suggest that Nkrankwanta pay allegiance to any traditional authority would not only be a request in poor taste, it would equally be a clear demonstration of the incorrect appreciation of Anyii Kotoko history. It could even be construed as an affront to the Kotoko stool.

A new chief swears to the people of Nkrankwanta to lead, defend, and protect the Kotoko stool as well as their heritage and integrity as a people. The entire ceremony is conducted in the Anyii Dwabene language because it is the medium with which to address the Kotoko stool and to also communicate with the ancestors. Perhaps the exception to the rule is when the talking drums summoning people to an important (usually grave) meeting intones, in Asante Twi, "Kotoko mo mra! Kotoko mo mra! Kotoko mo mra! Mo mra! Mo mra! Mo mra!" (People of Kotoko assemble! People of Kotoko assemble! People of Kotoko assemble! Assemble! Assemble! Assemble!). Also, most Anyii Dwabene war songs are sung in Twi, a clear throwback to the warrior background from the old days in Amansie and, to a greater degree, their immediate past as warriors who rescued Abron Bonduku from external aggression. A translation of the swearing in may be offered in Twi, primarily as a courtesy to special guests (who will include chiefs) and others who may not be conversant with the Anyii language. In any case, the average resident of Nkrankwanta understands and fluently speaks both Anyii and Twi.

After he has sufficiently settled in, the new chief embarks on a Nnaase (thank you) tour of his people and visits fellow chiefs in neighboring towns. This last gesture is to formally introduce himself to neighbor chiefs. The visits also afford the opportunity to develop closer ties between Nkrankwanta and her neighbors.

So far I have dwelt on enstoolment or coronation of a new chief to the Anyii Kotoko stool. I believe it is appropriate to discuss briefly the other side of the coin—namely the conditions and reasons for which a chief may be destooled. There has been one destoolment since Nkrankwanta was founded. Nana Kofi Asemia (Kofi Kra, in private life) was destooled for dissipating stool assets and also for being an absentee chief. He lived in Abidjan and could be gone for a whole year without visiting Nkrankwanta. He was briefly succeeded by Nana Kwame Adjei (he kept his own name), but Nana Kofi Asemia fought his way back to regain the stool. I will quickly note here that this discussion will not get into the details and reasons why Kwame Adjei abdicated and gave the throne back to Kofi Kra, except to say that though both men were from the same Ngesah Aku family, it was not an altogether voluntary decision.

A chief can be destooled or removed from office for improper behavior. The following acts, if proven, are improper behavior and therefore sufficient grounds for destoolment: knowingly having an affair with a married woman; stealing; engaging in a street brawl or fight; public drunkenness and behavior amounting to disgrace; failure to be a good custodian of stool assets; telling lies; being autocratic. This is a shortlist, but action or behavior deemed to have cast the Kotoko stool in a bad light or brought it into disrepute, if proven by witnesses before a council of elders, can be sufficient grounds for destoolment. Akan chiefs, and especially kings, are rarely destooled. This fact, however, does not mean that a traditional ruler among the Akan is immune from challenges to his leadership. On the contrary, knowing that there is the possibility of destoolment if he should behave badly is enough check for the incumbent to rule wisely and morally. In any event, a sitting chief's attention will be drawn to what he may be doing wrong before he gets really bad. And as has been mentioned earlier in this book, a chief among the Akan follows more instructions than he gives.

The destoolment process among the Anyii Dwabene is very simple. After the difficult decision has been made to destool a chief, which is the same as saving the sanctity and reputation of the stool in question, libation is poured, and the traditional sandals of the chief are removed from under his feet. I would like to quickly remind that a destooled chief, if a true royal, as distinct from a usurper, continues to enjoy some royal privileges for the fact that he once sat on the sacred stool and wore the sandals previous chiefs or kings used to wear, by virtue of which he was once liaison between the people and their ancestors. Also as chief or king, he represented the collective spirit and aspirations of the people.

Unlike Akan Twi-Fante, traditional administration among the Akan Anyii-Baulé is not structured on military hierarchy. This is perhaps because unlike Akan Twi-Fante, the respective histories of Akan Anyii-Baulé tribes have more to report on good neighborliness than on skirmishes and actual wars, or designs to annex neighbors. This explains why most wars in the histories of Anyii-Baulé tribes have been acts in self-defense against external aggression and have not lasted long enough to create or encourage a culture of military-type administrative structure.

In fact, many Akan Anyii-Baulé states were founded by groups that sought a new life away from familial misunderstandings that had led to implacable quarrels, drawn out infighting, and other forms of internal conflicts in the old country. Notable examples are the Baulé of Cote d'Ivoire who, in the eighteenth century and under the leadership of their matriarch and later queen, Abena Pokua, left Nsuta and Mampong areas of Asante to avoid infighting among branches of the same extended family. The Anyii Indenie, immediate southern neighbors to Anyii Dwabene, also migrated from Asante for the sake of peace. The principal town of the Indenie, Ampenkro (Ampε Nkro), a name that has been distorted by the French as Abengourou, is in Twi and loosely translates as "We dislike feuds." In other words, the Indinié were saying, "Enough of the infighting; we're leaving," and relocated from Nzandɛlɛ (Asante) to their new home.

In the epic migration story of Abena Pokua and her people, several sources have recorded that their opponents and detractors were in pursuit even as the breakaway group from Nsuta hurried away from old Asante, travelling westward. The narration continues that the group came upon a big and overflowing river. For fear their pursuers would catch up with them, the group decided to get to the other side of the river as quickly as they could. It was too dangerous to wade through the fast-flowing river, and the group had no boats or other means of conveyance to get them across. When the fetish priest travelling with the group consulted his oracle, he was informed that the river god had made a demand, following the fulfillment of which she would assist the group to cross to the other bank and to safety. The demand was a nonnegotiable one, and it was that Abena Pokua throw her only child travelling with the group into the fast-flowing river in sacrifice.

Abena Pokua thought long and hard; the maternal love in her dictated against deliberately causing the death of her child—and in this case, her only child. At the same time, the lives, safety, and collective welfare of her numerous followers depended on her decision and leadership. The matriarch took a few days to search her heart and ponder over the issue.

Finally, she arrived at a decision, and it was the most painful decision any parent, and especially a mother, would make: for the sake of her people, Abena Pokua decided to sacrifice her only child to the river god.

The narration continues that soon after Abena Pokua had thrown her child into the fast-flowing big river, an army of crocodiles lined up, jaw to tail, across the width of the river, forming a dangling reptilian bridge, upon which the Nsuta emigrants gingerly walked to safety. Henceforward, the group called itself "Baa Wule", meaning "The Child Died," hence Baulé. And when the Baulé have called themselves Wawulé, the name is derived from "Ye Wa Wule," which translates as "Her Child Died." Here again, in reference to the same event in history at the banks of the big, fast-flowing river, which many believe is the River Comoe. In sum, Abena Pokua sacrificed her only child for the sake of her people and the new Baulé nation. Whether a true story or legend, the Baulé celebrate Abena Pokua sacrificing her only child to the river god as a critical decision point in their history.

An artist's impression of Abena Pokua about to offer her child to the river god in sacrifice, an event in history that inspired a new nation called Baulé (baa wule meaning "the child died")

In spite of the numerous internal frictions and wranglings that forced most Akan Anyii-Baulé to emigrate, these have never stopped making references to their Nzandɛlɛ (Asante) roots. A few families still have contact with their ancestral extended families in Ghana and have been exchanging visits and marrying among themselves as a way of perpetuating shared blood relationships. And in a few cases where a stool or the position of family headship has become vacant, eligible candidates have been brought in from Nzandɛlɛ (Asante) to fill them up, and vice versa.

The fact Akan Anyii-Baulé tribes were generally not warlike does not mean they were pacifists. The fact Abron Bonduku sought out Anyii Dwabene warriors to liberate her from Bouna invasion is evident enough. Other examples of a call to arms include the War of Asikaso between Anyii Dwabene and French colonial forces, in which Yaw Fum, king of Dwabene, was clear aggressor. And in the nineteenth century, the Baulé mounted a couple Wars of Liberation against French colonialists.

Chapter 9

Identity and Heritage

A people disconnected from the umbilical chord that ties them to their history and heritage risk anonymity and, if not checked in time, cultural genocide. It is true regardless of national boundaries or geographical distance. It is also true that, like the proverbial domesticated eagle that was raised among chicks and that will some day rediscover itself and fly away into the wild where it naturally belongs, never to return, so will the bond between a people and its origins or roots, which cannot be broken permanently.

Contemporary society worldwide is replete with communities and peoples seeking to reestablish ties with their ancestral homes, and where these ties already exist, to strengthen them. In this regard, one may cite relations between Africans in the Diaspora and Black Africa, the various immigrant communities living in developed countries that are making strenuous efforts to reconnect with their ancestral or old countries for cultural and economic reasons, and the coming together of communities and tribal groups all over Africa that served different colonial masters. It is obvious that the growing interest to reconnect and, where they exist, strengthen historical ties with one's roots is a reality check that is at once necessary and natural, and it is that which cannot be denied, delayed, or frustrated. Closer to home, we observe with involved interest the strengthening of relations between Dormaaman and Akwamufie, the ancestral home of the people of Dormaa.

The Chokosi, a community located in the north of Togo that has been isolated from her Akan moorings in Ghana and Cote d'Ivoire for well over a century, continues to keep the flames of her Akanness burning in her heart. Chokosi may have taken on a new garb in language and other aspects of culture, yet she remains Akan in consciousness and worldview. Chokosi is but one community that reinforces the truism that ultimately a people separated by events in history will rediscover and embrace each other.

As if to echo the above sentiment, in recent years a few individuals have launched an all-Anyii cultural festival. Le Festival des Arts et de la Culture Agni (Festival of Anyii Arts and Culture) brings together all ten Agni subgroups to celebrate a common heritage and to cement historical ties. It is expected that the Festival will continue to grow in strength and reach, to include Anyii communities everywhere and perhaps link up with similar Akan-based organizations in Ghana because the Anyii are still very much conscious of their Ghanaian origins. It is not uncommon to read some Ivorian scholarly work referring to the Anyii as Agni-Achanti (Anyii-Asante). These scholars refuse to accept or embrace the fact that time and geographical distance in addition to the effects of different colonial systems and other cultural evolutionary dynamics have created a gap in linguistic and other cultural practices between the two once-unified Akan groups or communities.

A reminder about the objectives and activities of Le Festival Agni and what it may become as it expands and matures is the emphasis it will very likely place on the reality and oft-repeated saying among Anyii: "Though the English and French succeeded in drawing a physical frontier between us, there is no boundary between Anyii and Anyii."

Nana Boah Kwasi III (king of Anyii Indenie), Nana Anyini Bilé II (king of Anyii Dwabene), and Nana Amo Ndufo V (king of Anyii Sanvi), sharing the same stage at a Festival des Arts et de la Culture Agni celebration.

There is no better place to observe the real, and perhaps negative, effect of the separation of peoples by colonialists than at KofiBadukro (Badukro), a small Anyii Bonaa town in the Dormaa Traditional Area. The principal street of Badukro demarcates Ghana and La Cote d'Ivoire! It is interesting to watch couples or entire families crossing the "border" several times a day in order to live a normal life. Or, residents navigating two different and distinct legal systems, one based on French Napoleonic civil code, the other based on English common law, in order to resolve basic administrative issues. For the residents of Badukro, and others like them in border communities everywhere across West Africa, there can be no better alternative to the full implementation of the ECOWAS (Economic Community of West African States) protocol on the free movement of persons and goods.

Another classical example of a divided people is when one hears Half Assini, the name of a coastal town on the southwestern tip of Ghana that borders on Cote d'Ivoire. The obvious question that comes to mind on hearing the name of the town is, "Where is the other half?" When the English and French colonialists split up the Nzema, just like they did the Anyii and other frontier communities and peoples, a section of Nzema territory called Assini was split up almost in two equal halves. One half is in Cote d'Ivoire and is called Assinie while the other half is in Ghana and called Half Assini. It would be unreasonable and unethical to perpetuate a divided Assini, or any other community for that matter. Sadly, the map of Africa is still littered with communities and ethnic groups sliced into different countries as a result of European colonial interests.

Beside the celebration of a common ancestry and heritage, the strengthening of historical ties and relations building has engendered economic activities that have benefitted all. In the particular example of Nkrankwanta, linking up with other Anyii towns across the border in Cote d'Ivoire has brought tremendous economic benefits as well as enhanced subregional cooperation in the spirit of ECOWAS, or CEDEAO (Communauté Economique des Etats de l'Afrique de l'Ouest) in French. This last fact is evident on Friday "Market Day" at Nkrankwanta, where traders from Anyii Dwabene and as far away as Abengorou in Anyii Indenie country meet, do business, and bond with other traders from the following: Dormaa Ahenkro, Berekum, Takyiman, Sunyani, and Sampa (in Brong Ahafo Region); Adabokro, Debiso, Asanwinso, Bibiani, and Wiawso (in Western Region); Kumase and Bonwire, the traditional capital of the kente cloth (in Ashanti Region); and beyond.

One would hope for increased interaction and cooperation between Anyii Dwabene and Dormaaman, similar to what exists between Dwabene and Abron, even though the peculiar circumstances that gave rise to that relationship are not the same. If for no other reason, the mutual benefit in good neighborliness but also in the wider purpose and spirit of the free movement of people as enshrined under

ECOWAS protocols, make this argument reasonable and worth considering. It would be to the benefit of the two communities, who have mingled for reasons of geography and economic collaboration, dating back to the rubber trade period, and whose members are increasingly blurring the ethnic line through intermarriage. The traditional states of Dwabene and Dormaaman can lead the way in subregional cooperation and promotion of culture, trade, and commerce. Such an initiative would further cement the reality that the institution of chieftaincy is relevant to the modern nation state.

Already, there are a significant number of Dwabene and Dormaa communities living on each other's traditional land, not to mention growing intermarriages between members from both communities, to the extent that in many homes today, Anyii and Wam (Twi dialect spoken by the Dormaa) are spoken interchangeably as mother tongues. A call for greater cooperation between Anyii Dwabene and Dormaa is, therefore, a call for the formalization of the status quo.

The Intervening Years

Nkrankwanta had its first school in 1945, roughly thirty-two years following its founding. As is with first schools everywhere, the initial intake was for primary education, until it was progressively upgraded to offer senior elementary school curricula in subsequent years. Until independence in 1957 and the mass education policy of Kwame Nkrumah, Ghana's first president, most educational institutions were concentrated along the coast where Europeans had made first contact with the natives. Nkrankwanta got a senior high school in 1993, the Nkrankwanta Senior High/Technical School.

To some extent, the founding fathers of Nkrankwanta, though almost all had no formal education, had great foresight in their belief that the future of their town could not be divorced from the quest for education. For this reason, they not only pulled together resources to build a school block and hire a teacher in 1945, they invested in the education of their children. The decision to build a school at Nkrankwanta was not out of character of the Anyii, because by 1920, when most traditional rulers elsewhere had no formal education, Anyii Dwabene had crowned the educated Ndaa Kwasi king. Since then, all Dwabene kings have been lettered.

Equally commendable was the zeal with which the elders of Nkrankwanta competed to give the best education to their children, an opportunity they themselves had not had. Unfortunately, that generation (the third since the founding of Nkrankwanta) did not seem to have the foresight of their parents and instead failed to take advantage of the many educational opportunities that were available to them. There is no doubt this generation was a drawdown to the pursuit of human development at Nkrankwanta. The period was at the very height of the agitation for independence for the Gold Coast. There was no better time for a son of Anyii Kotoko, even with a high school diploma, to have impacted the liberation struggle of the day and, by it, the course of history. The third generation of Nkrankwanta squandered an irreparable opportunity for themselves and their town.

By the mid-1960s, Nkrankwanta had begun to assume administrative leadership among neighboring towns and villages. Though not yet of a constituency or municipal status, the town was effectively a subdistrict capital in police, education, and primary health care administration. "The Junction" had a Ghana Police post (later upgraded to a station), a resident director of education, and a health clinic. Also, because of its proximity to Cote d'Ivoire and status as a major cocoa-producing center, Nkrankwanta had become a virtual garrison town of rotating border patrol units serving the entire southwest region of Dormaa and especially, during the main cocoa harvesting season, to prevent smuggling across the border.

There was a moment in the history of Nkrankwanta, around the middle part of the twentieth century, when a significant number of Anyii converted, en masse, to Islam. Almost all the converts were of royal lineage, which means that a good number of the council of elders at the palace had, in one fell swoop, become Muslims. It is difficult to assign any specific reason for the mass conversion, but there is no doubt the collective decision was influenced by the long relationship between Nkrankwanta and Anyii Barebo from the time of Serekye Hejira, the Muslim scholar and holy man who had prepared a talisman at the request of the elders of Nkrankwanta so that their new town may grow in size and importance. Anyii Barebo country sits where the rain forest and Savannah meet in the north-central part of Cote d'Ivoire, immediately north of Anyii Bini and west of Abron Bonduku territories. Because of its proximity to Muslim kingdoms that lie immediately north of her—for example, the greater kingdom of Senoufo but in particular, the trading centers of Kong and Djimini—Barebo was influenced early by Muslim traders and scholars.

Among all Anyii groups, the Barebo were the first Muslim converts, to the extent that Anyii Barebo is Islamic in character. There used to be a standing joke among other Anyii subgroups, to the effect that if one wanted to see a circumcised male, one would have to make the long journey to Barebo country. The joke was in reference to the pervasive influence of Islamic culture among the Anyii Barebo, whose male members must circumcise as a requirement of their religion. That was the epoch during which male circumcision among most Anyii subgroups made one physically unwholesome, and if the person was of royalty, a disqualification to become chief or king. Female circumcision is alien to Anyii and the greater Akan culture.

My late grandmother narrated that when the royals of Nkrankwanta converted, the rest of the family did not take kindly to the idea and accused them of undermining their heritage and the Kotoko stool. Grandma Afua Seala (later, Hajia Masara Afua Seala) narrated that the new converts were ostracized and alienated, to the extent that a few left home for an extended period of time, and returned after the shock to the extended family had subsided somewhat, which permitted reconciliation. Ekyea Kaa (Ekyea Junior), from the Nziah Akpau lineage and son of Nana Yaa Pili, she who carried the Kotoko stool to Nkrankwanta, was of the first generation of Muslim converts at Nkrankwanta. Ekyea Kaa took the name Serekye (Sadiq) upon conversion and went on to learn more about Islam. He became the first Imam of Nkrankwanta. Today, members of the two royal houses of Anyii Kotoko are almost equally split between Islam and Christianity. They live in peace and harmony, as members of the same blood family.

Chapter 10

Nkrankwanta Today

Beloved

The town at the crossroads,
Also called the "Junction of Farewell."
The town, situationally situated,
Where tearful "au revoirs" were said.
"Bala ndɛ. Nyamea fa wɔ hɔ bala"
On the way to the coastline, the center, and grasslands.

And the town at the Junction,
Founded by the people who were "Mature at Birth."
A wise and wizened lot, they thought of themselves,
Brave warriors to the rescue of Abron Bonduku.

And the people,
They refused to bow, cower, or serve,
Strangers from the Bastille on Papa's land.

Zac Adama

And they left,
Left under threat, under duress,
So they came
And were received.

Physically separated from kindred,
Friendly neighbors abounding, though
Yet they were a lonesome lot,
Because blood is thicker than water.

They built a new settlement
And named it after the location
Young but growing fast
Like a bean stalk,
To the admiration of many
But the green-eyed envy of others.
Is the buried talisman secure?
That little bundle from Serekye Hejira
Purposed for the expansion of the new settlement.
'Twas Junction of Godspeed,
Presently a destination of Bienvenue,
Open arms for all, arrived and arriving.

Market Day is a beehive of activity.
Intra-border, cross-border, a veritable
Beacon of ECOWAS regional cooperation.
Friendship, barring none, spiting none.

Kotoko-So shall remain a daily reminder, always
shall.

You who're permanently clothed in Anyii Dwabene Kotoko,
Bonded, involuntarily, inseparably, to your past and kindred,
Even from behind frontier and administrations.

My beloved Junction town,
You who hold aloft the falcon staff of Oyoko,
You're cast for greatness and have a place in history.

In 2012, Nkrankwanta assumed administrative capital status of the newly created Dormaa West District and Constituency. The new status has brought tremendous growth in population size, infrastructural development, and economic activity to an already burgeoning agricultural and commercial town. From the transformation of a small rural settlement only a few decades ago into an increasingly urbanized town, the "The Junction" is a round-the-clock beehive of economic activity that would confound the wildest dreams and expectations of the founding fathers.

Market Day on Fridays and Sundays, but especially on Fridays, is a spectacle to behold. It is an event no serious trader within a three-hundred-mile radius can afford to miss: it is as if the entire West African subregion is on parade and showcasing its different product lines and cultures. Nkrankwanta is a place where agriculture and commerce thrive side by side, and seamlessly, too. Beside the display of varied products and cultural artifacts, Market Day is an agricultural show of sorts, where farmers feel an ultimate sense of pride and accomplishment in the produce they put on display and sale. Beside food crops, Nkrankwanta and area is a leading cocoa-producing part of Ghana. It is not for nothing that the capital of Dormaa West is sometimes referred to as "Cocoa Town."

It is often said that a visit to Nkrankwanta is a visit to all of West Africa. Not only is my beloved hometown a commercial and an agricultural town, the diversity of its population is a veritable microcosm of the subregion, with each group feeling at home and at peace. Destiny seems to have appointed Nkrankwanta a midwife of multiculturalism. The old Junction is the place where all are welcome and no one is made to feel a stranger; it is where all and sundry can call, and have called, home away from home.

Barely a generation ago, the intention of new settlers to Nkrankwanta, including many citizens of Dormaa, was to farm the land (mainly cocoa) and to return "home" once the farms had matured. With this in mind, many such newer arrivals did not invest in long-term and durable residential properties, reasoning that theirs would be a temporary stay only. But as Nkrankwanta became more and more commercialized and to some degree urbanized, the attitude of these communities has shifted to building homes for the long haul, and in the process, making Nkrankwanta their new and permanent hometown.

Like the founding fathers whose love for freedom and liberty propelled them to leave their original home of Kotokoso in search of new possibilities and opportunities, Nkrankwanta beckons to those in need of rest from travails as well as those who dare to dream and aspire to greater heights. Therefore, to say that Nkrankwanta is a town of immigrants, old, new, and arriving, is to state the obvious. And as is true of great towns and great nations everywhere, immigrants are the backbone or engine of growth, prosperity, and robust economic development. Therein lies the secret to Nkrankwanta's phenomenal growth and its continued attraction to newcomers. But to those who believe in the relevance and efficacy of the expansionist sumi of Nkrankwanta, the success story of Cocoa Town is according to the spiritual prescription of the buried talisman that Serekye Hejira, the spiritual man from Yorobodi in Anyii Barebo, produced. The story of Nkrankwanta is at once a story of fact, legend, and magic.

Whether by design or accident, Nkrankwanta seems destined to continually relive its history as the Ngwandaa (Twi: Nkwanta; junction or crossroads) of old, where people bade farewell on journeys they intended to return from. Only this time, the Junction has become a meeting point beckoning in Akwaaba (welcome), where it used to bid farewell and wish Godspeed. Also this time, people are not parting company or continuing to other locations. Instead, from all walks of life and in shared humanity, people have come to live in peace, security, and in the pursuit of prosperity amid abundant opportunities.

Echoes of the Future

Nkrankwanta will continue to grow in size and importance. There is no doubt about that. The town's reputation as a major food and cash-crop-producing hub, a robust commercial presence, and close proximity to Cote d'Ivoire have combined to make it a major attraction and draw for population influx from other parts of Ghana and the subregion as a whole. But perhaps the single most important factor to Nkrankwanta's continuous growth and accelerated development is the fact that it is in no competition with any other town within its immediate perimeter. None of the estimated 150 towns and villages within the geographical and administrative catchment of Nkrankwanta is large enough to attract equal attention in investment and developmental initiative. Rather, these smaller towns and villages together contribute toward Nkrankwanta's growth and economic importance. There is no doubt that Cocoa Town will continue to grow, carrying under its wing the banner of its relatively short but interesting and compelling history that has come to fulfill the hopes and aspirations of so many. Again, the history of Nkrankwanta will continue to be told, as it reveals itself more and more with renewed vigor and pleasant surprises.

I foresee a new Nkrankwanta with several

agro-based industries that will harness the abundant agricultural opportunities waiting to be exploited. I foresee a vibrant Cocoa Town increasingly diversifying into several economic activities without giving up its core agricultural base. I foresee an ever-ambitious Nkrankwanta reaching for the stars in educational infrastructure and skills training. And I foresee the Junction of old playing a more significant role in subregional integration because of the shared history and culture it enjoys with several communities across the border in Cote d'Ivoire. In this regard, Nkrankwanta could be an incubator for the implementation and realization of several ECOWAS protocols, policies, and projects.

But there is a danger that threatens to not only derail subregional economic development and cooperation but, worse, aims to shake the very foundations of the Kotoko stool. This ill-advised and careless move, if it goes unchecked, has the potential to disrupt the peaceful coexistence of the various ethnic communities at Nkrankwanta. It is a danger whose shadows have been lurking in the dark corners since Nkrankwanta assumed constituency and district capital status. It is as if some elements in society are losing their very essence since the elevation of Nkrankwanta to a higher political and administrative status. It seems these elements cannot stomach the steady progress and growing importance of Nkrankwanta.

I believe there is a solution, and it lies in education and the sharing of information. It is also important to make people aware that the success of Nkrankwanta is the success of all, since each and every resident and community benefits from it. I believe also that telling people the true story about Nkrankwanta will make them wiser and tolerant. Therefore, this book, *Cultural Migration: A Short History of Nkrankwanta and Anyii Dwabene*, is on a mission to inform, educate, and share knowledge, with the aim to assuage and mitigate the fear and perhaps envy, albeit unjustified, in the hearts and minds of some people.

Across Ghana, a few traditional seats have fallen victim to violence and destabilization. Nkrankwanta will not go the way of these towns. She will stand united and firm and preserve the peace she has enjoyed within herself, with neighbors and the wayfarer, since from when she was founded in 1917. Nkrankwanta shall prevail as a united and peaceful town.

Be not caught up in the wind,
Of destructive inkling.

A quarrelsome mind
Is fickle and in a bind.

Just don't mind.

The truth must be told—and told early. Otherwise, untruth shall be accorded undeserved attention and respect, however fleeting or temporary. A short time span, especially in a charged atmosphere, is sometimes all evil minds need to sow disunity where there has been absolute unity, breed hatred where love has ruled supreme, and cause destruction and havoc where continuous development has been the way of life. If unchecked, the evil-minded will divide, destroy, and quietly disappear into the night, leaving behind broken relations to be mended by others, perhaps over generations, if at all possible. But as one Akan proverb puts it, "Some objects, when dropped, can be picked up or recovered; not so other objects." For example, palm nuts can be picked up or recovered when dropped from a container, but not so palm oil, yet both objects are from the same product source. In context, it is more advisable, easier, and wiser to prevent harm, chaos, or tragedy than to attempt to find solutions after the fact.

Nana Anyini Bilé II, king of Anyii Dwabene,
seated during a state function

Nana Agyeman Badu II, king of Dormaaman, sits in state

A primary objective of the publication of *Cultural Migration: A Short History Nkrankwanta and Anyii Dwabene* will be met if violence is averted because of knowledge gained through its pages. The fascinating story about the founding history of the Junction is equally important to explore. Above all, I intend this work to be among efforts at promoting peace through the power of good information and knowledge derived therefrom.

Earlier in this book, I proposed a cultural partnership between Dormaaman and Anyii Dwabene, similar to what has existed between Dwabene and Abron, dating back almost three centuries. Though the historical background to the proposal may not be as far-reaching as between Dwabene and Abron, the simple fact of permanent neighborliness is sufficient enough reason to foster a closer cultural and economic relationship. And in pursuit of that relationship, there is no doubt that Nkrankwanta will play a central role. But a litmus test in that initiative will be the level of friendship between tenant Anyii Kotoko, namely Nkrankwanta, and landlord Dormaaman, because at a minimum, Nkrankwanta is the face of Anyii Dwabene across the border in Ghana.

The position of Nkrankwanta in Anyii Dwabene hierarchy makes it difficult to absorb her fully into another paramountcy. Nkrankwanta simply cannot be subordinate to another stool and expect to play its proper role as second most senior stool in Anyii Dwabene state. At the same time, it will be problematic for Nkrankwanta to assume the status of paramountcy on somebody else's land. What then should be a workable middle-ground solution?

I propose the following. On the one hand, the host landlord must be assured that any arrangement will not challenge or encroach on his authority. On the other, the settler community would not like to be reduced to a status that will make it difficult to maintain a level of independence necessary to play its proper role as a senior member of Anyii Dwabene. But there must be a solution, one that is beneficial to generations of both communities—and, more importantly, a solution that will guarantee continuous peace. In the final analysis, I see Nkrankwanta as playing the role of cultural midwife. The future role of Anyii Kotoko in this regard can be described in the following solution proposal.

Nkrankwanta can be granted a semiautonomous traditional status that will make it a useful liaison between Dormaaman and the rest of Anyii Dwabene. If properly implemented and managed, the enhanced status of Nkrankwanta will foster greater friendship and cooperation between Dormaa Ahenkro and AnyiniBilékro—a situation that will benefit all, culturally and economically. On the other hand, subterfuge, coercion or chicanery will not benefit Dormaaman or Anyii Kotoko.

This is the story of Ngala Ngwandaa, my beloved hometown.

Chapter 11

A Window into Anyii
Culture and Society

Spirituality, Belief System, and Godhead

"Nyamea" in Anyii and "Nyame" in Twi is God Almighty. Nyamea is Creator God of all beings and things and lives somewhere in the sky, above the clouds. He is often called "Nyamea Pili" (Nyame Kɛseɛ or Nyame Kokroko in Twi). The "Pili" is in reference to his unbounded grandeur and power. He is also Nana Nyamea, more than deserving of the honorific "Nana" reserved for kings, chiefs, and grandparents. Nyamea is the omniscient, omnipotent Almighty God who sees all, hears all, and is everywhere. So when it is said among the Twi that "wo a, wo hunta dua akyi, sɛ obi anhunu wo a, Nyame ahunu wo" (you who are hiding behind a tree, you must be deluded in thinking no one sees you, because God does), the message is that no activity, however insignificant, remote, or obscure, escapes the effortless knowledge and comprehension of Nyamea, or Nyame.

Nyamea or Nyame has no form; he does not look like anybody, and none looks like him. Anyii and other Akan approach and address Nyamea in two ways—directly by way of the spoken word and indirectly through intercessory, third-party agents. Speaking directly to the Most High, one would often hear this very common expression of gratitude among Anyii and other Akan: "Nyamea yila wɔ" ("Nyame nhyira wo" in Twi), meaning "God bless you." Or "Nyamea boka me" ("Nyame boa me" in Twi), a plea to God for help, meaning "God help me." One very common expression among them all when someone has been wronged is this: "fa ma Nyamea" ("fa ma Nyame" in Twi), an advice to "leave everything in the hands of God"; in other words, "forgive him/her." No well-spoken Akan will announce doing something in the future without the God-dependent statement "Wɔ yɛ Nyamea fɛ a …," or "Nyamea boa a …" in Anyii, and "Onyame pɛ a …" in Twi, meaning "God willing …" In other words, God Almighty determines and rules over one's life. The surrender to God's driver role among the Akan is irrespective of one's religious affiliation. It is obvious that among the Akan, belief in a Creator God and one's relationship with, or dependence on, Him predates the arrival of the Muslim preacher or Christian missionary.

At the same time, Anyii and other Akan believe that because of his grandeur, power, and authority, and just as one does not directly address a chief or king except through a spokesperson, one communicates with Nyamea or Nyame through one of several intercessory agents. These agents are usually the spirits believed to inhabit natural objects and to whom offerings are made "for onward transmission" for the purposes of expiation, intercession, or gratitude. Such objects are typically out of the ordinary as in, for example, powerful rivers, mountains, and unusual natural formations. It is also believed that the spirits behind those objects can themselves resolve minor issues and problems that may afflict an individual or the community as in, for example, the invocation of a god to identify, curse, or punish a thief or some other wrongdoer.

Ancestors are invoked in this manner to decide in matters of dispute or contention. So is Aseɛ (Anyii), Asase (Twi), or Mother Earth. Invocations are usually done by pouring libation while speaking to them or making the offering of an animal or food items for the spirit on call. Adherents believe that the gods and intercessor spirits respond quickly to requests for assistance and protection. Contact with the gods is usually made through fetish priests and other seers.

The Odum tree (botanical: *Chloiphora excelsa*) has a special place in the belief system among Akan people, especially as it relates to offering sacrifices to gods and spirits. It is generally believed that a mature Odum is inhabited by spirits. The belief, therefore, is that leaving offerings at the base of an Odum yields quick, if not instant, results, by virtue of the fact that spirits are already present. Odum in

Twi is the colloquial name for Dui, the same as Elui among Anyii-Baulé tribes. Perhaps the significance of the spiritual nature of the Odum tree is why several towns are called Odumase (Twi for "at the base of Odum"), or Elubo in Anyii-Baulé, which means the same thing.

While it may seem that traditional Anyii and Akan belief systems relate more to tactile forms, it is also true to say that individuals have a profound and direct relationship with the unseen and untouchable Nyamea or Nyame on a daily basis. It is not uncommon to hear the expression "sɛ wɔyɛ Nyamea fɛ a ..." (Anyii), or "sɛ Nyame pɛ a ..." (Twi) prefixing a statement to do something in the future. In translation, "God willing" is basic protocol in proper Anyii and Akan statement when one intends to do something in the future.

Though the Akan belief system recognizes that there is life after death, the afterlife is not the same as pertains in Abrahamic religious belief. Akan belief holds that the dead live in an out-of-world community called "Nwomee Kulo" in Anyii and "Nsamanfo ɔ Kurom" or "Asamando" in Twi, where none dies again. Nwomee Kulo or Asamando simply means "town/city/community of ghosts." Heaven and hell, where one lives in perpetual bliss surrounded by unimaginable beauty and opulence, or is condemned to a life of pain and misery in a blazing inferno, are alien to traditional Akan belief. Consequently, the belief in a judgment day on which Nyamea or Nyame will sit in judgment on one's deeds while on earth does not exist in the Akan belief system. Similarly, angels are an unknown creation in traditional Akan belief. Reward and punishment for one's actions are dealt with during one's earthly life, where one will either suffer pain or an affliction or be surrounded by love and happiness.

The Akan, like most other African peoples, are spiritual by default. Virtually all worldly activities, happenings, and events have spiritual undertones; they are driven or influenced by one or other behind-the-scene supernatural agent or reason. Throughout the discussion on spirituality, I have referred to an Akan belief system instead of religion, because there is no indigenous Akan religion. Though it shares in spirituality with a belief system, a religion has the following additional basic attributes: derives its origin and inspiration from a historical person or persons with a unique message about a way of life; is a movement for, or revolutionizes, social change; has a written set of code, methods, rules, and regulations; often has a uniform structure in rites and liturgy; membership is driven by a common, shared spiritual goal; seeks a universal outlook and reach; has a hierarchy of leadership and authority; and has otherworldly judgment between good and evil, and reward and punishment. By contrast, the traditional Akan belief system consists of a pantheon of gods and intermediary spirits and an unwritten code or rules. It is less structured and less organic and has a more liberal approach to worship and spirituality. However, the Akan belief system shares with organized religion in the knowledge about a Creator God and the need to defer to Him.

The Family

The concept of family among the Anyii and indeed all Akan is the extended, communal definition, as distinct from the nuclear family consisting primarily of wife, husband, and children. Even with urbanization and the high demands of the money economy, the African family concept has not changed very much. By extended definition means the Anyii define family beyond the household to include all blood relatives, generations up and down. Adopted children are also part of family. The extended family is the primary cell of socialization among Anyii.

Several families of the same genealogy constitute what the Anyii and all other Akan call "abusua." In its proper definition and character, the system of abusua transcends the close-knit structure of the immediate family. The abusua system transcends tribe, which means that each Akan tribal group may consist of more than one abusua. I have identified the eight Akan abusua in an earlier chapter, but for brevity of this discussion and ease of reference, I reproduce the list here:

	Abusua Name	Akyenaboa (Insignia or Totem)
1.	Aduana (a.k.a. Atwea, Abrade, Amoakare ne Ada)	Dog
2.	Asona	Crow
3.	εkoɔna (a.k.a. Kwɔnnafo, εkoɔ ne Asimpi. Ahweniε a εda yaawa mu, Asɔkɔrefoɔ)	buffalo (Anyii=εhoε; Twi=εkoɔ)
4.	Bretuo ne Tena (Fantse—Twidanfo)	Leopard
5.	Agona (Fantse—Eguanafo)	Parrot
6.	Asenie (Fantse—Atwafo)	Bat
7.	Asakyiri (a.k.a. Amoakaadefoɔ. Fantse—Anonafo)	Hawk
8.	ɔyɔko (Yɔkofo or Dehyena in Fantse)	Falcon

I mentioned that every Akan must belong to one of eight abusua extended families. Membership of an abusua is an obligation; one is obligated by accident of birth. The concept is best expressed in the Twi proverb: "Abusua nyɛ sa, na wa bɔ agyae" (Membership of an abusua is unlike joining the military, where one can sign up for or retire from).

Among Anyii and also all Akan, there is no word distinction between siblings—namely brothers, sisters, half brothers, half sisters, or cousins. All are brothers or sisters. "Aniama" in Anyii, or "Onua" in Twi can refer to a brother, sister, half brother, half sister, and cousin. "Aniama" and "Onua" can further be broken down into "Aniamabala" or "Onuabaa" to refer to a female sibling of this family category. Also, "Aniamabiésua" or "Onuabarima" refers to a male sibling. The simplified sibling relationship among the Anyii and all other Akan tribal groups further reinforces the abusua concept where family is similar to clan relationship in other cultures.

Wɔfa is both Anyii and Twi for uncle, except that among Akan, uncle is restricted to a male brother to one's mother. Here also, a mother's brother includes her half brothers and cousins. In typical Akan family classification, a brother to one's father is either a junior father (*seɛ kaa/seɛ kutuwa* in Anyii and *agya kuma* in Twi) or senior father (*seɛ kpai* in Anyii and *agya panin* in Twi), depending whether that male relative is younger or older than one's father. A father's brother is never a wɔfa, or an uncle. Again, a father's brothers include half brothers and cousins. A maternal aunt (mother's sister—that is, blood sisters and cousins) is *mmo kaa* in Anyii and *éno kumaa* in Twi if younger than one's mother, and *mmo kpai* in Anyii and *éno panin* if older. Direct translation of mmo kaa or éno kumaa is younger mother, while mmo kpai or éno panin means senior mother. A father's sister is also *mmo kaa* or *mmo kpai* in Anyii, but *sowaa/ sewaa* in Twi. A grandmother or grandfather is Nana.

In downward relationships, an *awosoa/awosea* in Anyii and *wɔfaase* in Twi (gender neutral; nephew or niece) is son or daughter to one's sister from the mother's side of family. The awosoa/awosea or w ɔfaase will address one as wɔfa, namely uncle. Interestingly, children from one's brother from either side of the family and sister from the father's side are one's children, but children from a sister on the maternal side are nephews and nieces, awosoa/ awosea or wɔfaase. It is evident the matrilineal Akan, which includes the Anyii, place emphasis on a sister's children in their complex family organizational structure.

The obvious preference accorded awosoa/ awosea or wɔfaase (nephews and nieces) in traditional Akan social cell organization speaks to the matrilineal inheritance system, up to and including stool occupant eligibility. Perhaps the Akan believe that there is greater blood certainty about a child issued from a sister's womb than one from a brother's wife. Akan society unquestionably and fully accepts the bias toward a maternal sister's children in matters of inheritance. After all, the same Akan philosophize in Twi, "ɔpemfoɔ na onim ne ba se" (none knows the father of a pregnant woman's baby better than herself).

Though Akan and for that matter Anyii society is matrilineal, the head of family (*awulo kpai* in Anyii and *abusuapanin* in Twi) is male. It is reasonable to conclude that the matrilineal structure of Akan culture and inheritance is so in order to leave no doubt about the blood origins of family headship and stool occupancy. The Twi say that "ɔbarima yɛ na" (a male is a prized asset), but never "ɔbaa yɛ na" in the same sense as a male because among the Akan, the male not only has primary responsibility of raising children of the abusua, he provides for and protects the family, and in times of national emergency, defends or fights in the cause of the nation. The Akan woman, on her part, is the supporting source of strength to her male relative. In traditional Akan society, therefore, there is distribution of labor and specialization of roles that leave no doubts in the minds of members of society.

The fact that the head of family is male among the Akan does not preclude women from exercising decision-making and leadership roles. In fact, a few women have not only led their people to found kingdoms, some have dragged and led reluctant male compatriots onto the battlefield. When the British defeated the Asante kingdom in 1900 and proceeded to humiliate Nana Agyeman Prempeh I, the reigning king of Asante, it was Yaa Asantewaa, queen mother of ɛdweso (Ejiso), who commandeered the chiefs and other notables of Asante to not sit idle by while their king was being humiliated. It is even reported that Nana Yaa Asantewaa had to invoke the sacred oath of Asante before she could get the mainly male chiefs and notables to follow her to war against the powerful British Army. Though Yaa Asantewaa was defeated and later taken prisoner and exiled to the Indian Ocean island of Seychelles along with King Agyemang Prempeh I, where she died, she had shown strong-willed decision making and bravery on the battlefield as most male compatriots shook in cowardice.

In nation building and political leadership, there are a few examples where female leaders led their people to found new kingdoms or ruled existing ones. For example, Nana Afia Dokua ruled Akyem Abuakwa from 1817 to 1835. Abena Pokua led her people from Mampong Nsuta in present-day Ghana to migrate and found the kingdom of Baulé in present-day Cote d'Ivoire. Nana Dwaben Serwaa led her people from Asante Dwaben to establish the new kingdom of New Dwaben in present-day south-central Ghana, where she ruled wisely and effectively.

Betrothal and Marriage

Arranged marriage exists in traditional Anyii society. It is called *asiwa*, the same as in Twi-speaking Akan. Asiwa refers more to a future bride than bridegroom and conveys the message of "she has been taken." Etymologically, asiwa is most likely a derivative of *asi awowa*, which translates as "reserved." And indeed the two young sweethearts have been reserved, each waiting impatiently for a day in the near future when they will be joined in formal matrimony. Asiwa is when two families pair a male and female child from opposite sides as a future couple. The two families make the decision with little or no input from the future couple. Where input is sought, it's perfunctory, often limited to asking either future couple whether they like each other. And for two minors to make as far-reaching decision as partner eligibility and marriage, one might as well say that their respective families should decide for them.

The most likely pairing for the purpose of asiwa among Anyii, and indeed among all other Akan groups, is between cousins, of any degree. When society was more communal and revolved around hunting and subsistence agricultural economy, the Akan found wisdom in keeping wealth within the bloodline. Therefore, when two cousins enter into matrimony, they not only perpetuate the bloodline, they also keep landed property and other assets within the larger family. These include land, farms, gold, and other marketable valuables.

The engaged do not share the same living quarters following asiwa and are expected to abstain from sexual intercourse until they are officially married. For the future bride, marriage readiness is when she has gone through the *nzuénu* ceremony, a rite of passage that ushers her into womanhood. Meantime, the asiwa will go through homemaking skills and parental training, both at home with her mother and at the house of her future mother-in-law, where she will get to learn a few things about her future husband, including his likes and dislikes. For the future bridegroom, it is common practice to occasionally help his future in-laws on the farm and with traditional male-defined tasks, such as repairing the family house. The pair is expected to show respect and kindness to their respective parents-in-law as they help with housework or farm work.

Though parents will more likely pair a boy and a girl in an asiwa relationship, the ultimate decision to marry or not marry each other rests with the two. Indeed, there have been several examples where the individuals in the arranged relationship, having grown up, have decided to marry someone else they met along the way and found more compatible than their reserved childhood partner. With education, travel, urbanization, the money economy, social media, and other contact points on the Internet, asiwa as a first step on the road to matrimony among the Anyii and other Akan groups is no longer in vogue. However, irrespective of the trappings of modernity, cousins are encouraged to marry if they develop love for each other, independent of prior parental or family intervention.

Marriage is not between two individuals; it is a bond between two families. As such, relatives become involved in the lives of the couple. The following Akan proverb vividly captures the marriage as a bond between two families and abusua:

Aboa bi pɛ éfié aba a, na ɔbɛ sisi sumpinaso
Obi pɛ abusua mu aba a, na ɔba mu awadeɛ

Meaning: it is the wild animal that longs for living among humans that forages on dumpsters on the edge of town. Similarly, it is the man who wants to be part of a particular family that chooses a woman from that family.

It is obvious from the above proverb that in typical Akan worldview, it is the male that takes the first step in the courting and marriage process. The female, on her part, reacts or responds to a man's courting and marriage proposal. This is assuming the relationship did not originate from asiwa betrothal where, generally speaking, parents from opposite sides initiate and manage the process.

If marriage is not by asiwa betrothal, a man interested in a woman will send an emissary to inform the family of the woman he has fallen in love with and intends to marry. The party will present an unspecified amount of cash and other presents to the woman's parents. The point of contact of intended bride will be her father, if alive, or a male representative from her father's family. The future bride's father will formally inform her mother, who may know about this already. This first step in the process is called *k ɔkɔɔkɔ* (typifying a knock on the door), where a man introduces himself and breaks the news to the family of a woman he intends to marry. The emissary will depart and expect a response from the woman's family in a few days' time. In the background, the woman's father or parents will inform other members of the larger family about the news. They will also conduct investigations about their daughter's suitor. After obtaining their daughter's consent, the family will send word to their future son-in-law saying they have received his message and accepted the prenuptial gifts. This indicates consent to him marrying their daughter.

There are few occasions when a woman's parents may reject a suitor's proposal to marry their daughter. This includes if there is historical bad blood between the opposite family lines or if the bride's parents, through background investigations, find the young man not a suitable partner to give away their daughter to. The parents' decision in the affair reminds that they will not sign onto an enterprise that has the potential to make their daughter unhappy or drag the family name into disgrace and disrepute. If the source of rejection is as a result of historical bad blood, representations and amends can be made to iron out whatever difficulties took place in the past, and bridge the chasm between the two families. But it is very unlikely a responsible family will give the hand of a daughter to a man with a known bad character or a questionable personal background, in which case the suitor's presents will be returned. After all, the Akan have a saying: "Nyanzoa/Animguaseɛ mvata Kan-Nia baa" (Anyii) and in Twi, "Animguaseɛ mfata Kan-Ni ba" (It is only proper for an Akan to live above shame and disgrace).

Assuming the bride's parents accept to give the

hand of their daughter in marriage, a day will be set for the marriage ceremony. As always, the ceremony will be an event between two extended families, that of the bride and the bridegroom. After preliminary greetings and introductions, the convener of the gathering, usually the *abusuapanin* (clan head) or even the chief of the town will announce the purpose of the meeting. Typically, the chief will address the gathering through his linguist or spokesperson (*kyaame* in Anyii; *okyeame* in Twi), in accordance with protocol. A spokesperson representing the family of the bridegroom will be asked to state the *amaneε* why they were at the grand meeting. Among the Akan, a guest, visitor, or one returning from a trip will go round to greet host, family, and kindred. He will be given a seat and served water, after which he will be greeted back with "akwaaba," meaning welcome. The guest or returnee will be asked the amaneε, which is an inquiry about the purpose of visit or to relate information about the trip he is returning from.

In this instance, the spokesman for the bridegroom's family will submit to the audience an amaneε to the effect that his male relative wants to take Miss So-and-So for wife. In due respect to the family that has raised such a beautiful and well-cultured person, he would be at great fault to not ask permission and the blessings of the family of Miss So-and-So to grant him the privilege to share his life with their daughter. The amaneε will typically say something about the bridegroom, including his hometown (if he is not from the same town as his future wife), who his parents are, where he lives, what he does for a living, and a few other pieces of personal information. After his amaneɛ, the spokesman for the bridegroom will thank the elders and everybody gathered for listening to him and return to his seat.

The convener of the meeting or presiding elder will thank the spokesperson and give a short speech, typically extolling the values their daughter was raised with and about the challenges of married life in general. He will invite comments from the audience, after which he will turn to the bride and ask the question: "Our dear daughter, we are gathered here today because this young man over there," may call him by name, "has brought us these drinks, asking for your hand in marriage. Should we accept his drinks?"

The answer to the question is rarely no. After the bride has given consent, the elders will pour drinks and pass it around for a sip. In like manner, a woman seeking divorce from her husband will "return his drink" to the man's family. A speaker for the bridegroom, on behalf of family, will thank the elders and family of the bride. In fact, the delegation from the bridegroom's family will go around shaking hands, amid "yɛ da amɔ ase" and "yɛ yɔ amɔ mmo" in Anyii, or "yɛ da mo ase" and "yɛ ma mo ammo" in Twi, in thanksgiving and gratitude.

In addition to the drinks, the party representing the bridegroom will typically present cash to the bride's parents and aunts, a gesture of gratitude for having raised a daughter with the qualities of a good wife. And for the bride, the audience will be shown a range and an assortment of gifts and valuables from her husband and in-laws. The gifts will include cash, traditional cloths, footwear, and homemaking items and gadgets. The gifts for the bride constitute what is colloquially called the bride price.

*A young Anyii woman dressed in gold and
gold dust ceremonial ornaments*

Among Anyii and other Akan tribes, the bride price is not a purchase price of the woman or her rights as a person; nor does it in any way, form, or shape place her under bondage during marriage. After all, among the Akan, women can, and do, "return drinks" in unworkable marriages. When women have to make the difficult decision of divorce, tradition does not oblige them to return other items the bridegroom presented at marriage. Even with the drinks being returned, they do not have to be the exact quantity, quality, or cost as those presented at marriage. A symbolic gesture of drinks to the bridegroom's family and a statement to the effect the bride is seeking divorce suffice. The bride price simply is a token recognition given to the parents and all who played a role in the raising of a girl child into a responsible woman and a principal source of a future generation. It is often the case that the bride's family will bargain for more in the value of a bride price, citing, for example, the woman's family background or other social statuses. For the well heeled and deep-pocketed, the matrimonial gifts can be anybody's guess. If the bride is of royalty or has higher education, the bride price and gifts come commensurate with her social status.

A male relative to the bride, usually a brother (in all the senses according to Akan definition of brother) will be appointed and introduced as intervener and moderator in matters of disputes and conflict resolution between the new couple. The common reference to this person role in Twi is *akonta sekan*, where "akonta" ("akonda" in Anyii) means brother-in-law and "sekan" means, literally, a double-edged knife or machete. The symbolism is that the appointed male intervener and moderator relative will understand his sister and also brother-in-law well enough to make impartial judgment in the event of a matrimonial dispute. The scenario is expressed as a proverbial two-edged sword that cuts both ways without favor.

Among Anyii and indeed all Akan, biological parents are the last resort in matrimonial conflict resolution, perhaps because of the emotional attachment biological parents, and especially mothers, have to their sons or daughters involved in difficult marriage situations. Traditionally, Akan believe that it is very unlikely a parent-in-law and especially a mother-in-law will be an impartial arbiter in a conflict situation involving her son or daughter. The belief is that maternal instincts will more likely than not stand in the way of objectivity and impartiality.

At this point, the presiding elder will offer pieces of advice to the new couple. He will then invite any from the audience who want to say a few words. It should be noted that except for when the bride is asked to inform whether or not her family should accept the drinks her suitor presented, neither of the couple speaks throughout the rest of the ceremony.

The last statement of the Akan marriage ceremony, which many in contemporary society find not only unfair and annoying but discomforting and even insulting, is best expressed in Twi. The elder representing the family of the bride will say, in exact words, "Yɛn ba a, yɛ de no ama wo awadeɛ nnɛ yi, sɛ ɔnya ade a, ɔde bɛ ba fie. Na mmom sɛ ɔnya ɛka a, ɛyɛ wo de a."

In full interpretation, it means "Today, we have given the hand of our daughter to you in marriage. From this moment on, she is your wife. In the course of the marriage, she will bring to her extended family all benefits that will accrue to her. However, you will be solely responsible for all expenditures and debts that she may incur."

Taken at face value, the last statement made at traditional marriage among Akan is a veritable nuptial insult to the male spouse. But a closer analysis of the statement reveals a fundamental truth. In Akan worldview, the most important item on the scale of wealth measurement is the size and influence of family. For a culture that is matrilineal, a culture in which one traces one's roots and traditional inheritance on the mother's side of the equation, wealth is measured by the size and influence of the maternal line of one's family. By this worldview, the woman and her family are net beneficiaries because children born in the marriage belong to her family more so than to her husband's. It is not uncommon to hear an elderly Akan woman lamenting, "I don't have a child," when, in fact, she may have given birth to a son. By such or similar statement, the "birth mother who has never given birth" is saying that her grandchildren, from the traditional standpoint, will belong to the family or abusua of his daughter- or daughters-in-law.

The following proverb makes the best statement about the human being as most important asset in traditional Akan society: "Sikaa yε nyeme, koso w ɔ ndo swana" (Anyii); "Sika yε fε, εnso εnto onipa" (Twi). It means, "There is no wealth higher or more valuable than the size of one's blood relatives."

On the issue of a husband being solely responsible for all of his wife's expenditures and debts, it is true that no husband worth the name will run to his in-laws expecting them to feed, clothe, and house his wife or bear other expenses, including cost of restoring her health in the event of sickness. In effect, the Akan speak truthfully even as they seem annoyingly blunt regarding the nuptial insult to the male spouse.

Akan culture permits a man having more than one wife. Even with urbanization, the money economy, and the desire of every parent to send their children to school, men who can afford to take good care of more than one wife and their children do practice polygamy. For most of the women who consent to being the other wife, the conventional wisdom is that there is more security and respect being a married woman than as a concubine or girlfriend. And if she has an out-of-wedlock pregnancy or child with the man in question, a woman in Akan society will very likely better ensure the well-being and security of her child within marriage than outside of it.

Akan culture does not allow performance of traditional marriage ceremony if the intended bridegroom is pregnant. The appropriate ceremony in this case is the first step, kɔkɔɔkɔ, the knock on the door, which is the same as when an intended bridegroom gives respect by officially introducing himself to the woman's parents. The main reason Akan culture rejects the performance of a full marriage ceremony is that doing so would be compelling the two parties to marry when, in fact, they may not have been ready had the woman not become pregnant. However, the two will be encouraged to perform the full traditional marriage ceremony after the woman has delivered.

Birth and Naming

As head of family, a husband has the prerogative or first right to choose a name for his newborn. Anyii and other Akan usually name their babies after parents and other relatives, dead and alive. The practice ensures keeping names of significant members of one's family in memory. In this regard, a couple may keep in memory names of a few living and late relatives who have touched their lives or the lives of the community, and sometimes the nation at large. The following Twi proverb fully captures the child-naming practice in the larger Akan culture: "Saman pa na wɔ gu no nsa. Saman pa na wɔ to no abadin." Or, "It is the good and deserving ancestor whose spirit is invoked during pouring of the libation. Similarly, babies are named after good and deserving ancestors," where good and deserving are interpreted as upright qualities that make one looked up to.

An Akan father will typically name his first newborn after his mother or grandmother, if a female, and his father or grandfather, if the baby is male. He will also name some of his children after key individuals from his spouse's family. For this reason, it is not uncommon to meet siblings having different names. Traditional Akan culture does not have family names. Also, traditional Akan society identifies an individual by the larger abusua classification. Where it is necessary to identify at the micro level, reference to hometown, lineage, parents, or the father-child naming convention known among Anyii and other Anyii-Baulé Akan becomes appropriate.

As with Twi-Fante, every Anyii-Baulé newborn is named after somebody in the family, living or dead. This I will call the baby's "proper" or maiden name as distinct from a surname because it is not a surname in the proper sense of Western culture, where typically a surname is the last name of the male parent. A baby among the Akan has a name by default, indicating the day on which he or she was born. I will call this a "day name." Among Akan Twi-Fante, this is almost always a first name. For example, the boy name Kofi is because the child was born on a Friday (Efieda). If female, the girl name would be Afua or Afia. Akua is girl name for a female child born on a Wednesday (Wukuada). The corresponding boy name is Kwaku.

But among Anyii-Baulé, a day name is sometimes the proper name. Therefore, when somebody wants to know which Kofi or Akua is being discussed, that person's father's name comes into play. For example, we find among the Anyii common names like Kofi Kwaku, Kofi Kofi, or even Kofi Akua! The common name seems to be set in a question-and-answer format, such as, "Whose son or daughter is he or she?" Then, "Oh! That is Kwaku's son or Kofi's daughter." So one conversant with Anyii-naming convention, on hearing the names Ekyea Yaa and Ekyea Ama, for example, will readily know that Yaa and Ama are daughters of Ekyea and are therefore siblings.

The arrangement of my name is a good example of person names according to Anyii culture and usage. When Grandpa Kwasi Pili converted to Islam, he took the name Adama (a West Africanized distortion of Adam). "Vieux" (Old man) Adama, partriarch of the family from Kongodja at Dame, Cote d'Ivoire, named one of his children Zaccharia, my father. Grandpa died a few years before I was born. Dad said he was the favorite among his father's children; if not for any other reason, he was the spitting image of his father, and available photographs attest to that. Father named me after Nana Adama Kwasi Pili. As by Anyii naming convention, therefore, my late father's name was Adama Zaccharia (Adama's son), and I am Zaccharia Adama (Zaccharia's son). Similarly, grandpa is sometimes remembered as Angama Kwasi Pili because his father's, and my paternal great-grandfather's, name was Angama.

Some Anyii in recent times and in line with this

usage have qualified their names or the names of their children with the possessive *wa*, which means "child of" or "offspring of" in Anyii. If this option had been chosen, my father would have been Adama wa Zaccharia, and I, Zaccharia wa Adama.

Anyii and Akan naming convention seems the exact opposite of what pertains in Western and some other cultures, where the name of the male family head is often given not only to his direct descendants but adopted by women married into his family—as in, for example, Mrs. Smith or Mrs. IamSomebody'sWife. Traditional Anyii and indeed Akan culture does not require of a woman to take the surname of her husband. Though Owurayere (Twi for Mrs.) often refers to a married woman in Ghana, the title or honorific is a later adaptation and inheritance of the colonial heritage. In this regard, women in traditional Akan society were liberated long before their sisters in Western and other societies.

Although the Anyii have different names for the days of the week, day or *kra da* names follow Akan Twi-Fante usage. The table below compares Anyii names for the days of the week to those of Twi, and the same male and female kra da child names associated with those days.

	Day Name (Anyii)	Day Name (Twi)	Female Child (Anyii)	Female Child (Twi)	Male Child (Anyii)	Male Child (Twi)
Monday	KiSié	Dwoada	Adwa	Adwoa	Kwadwo	Kwadwo
Tuesday	Dwɛlɛ	Benada	Abana (nasal)	Abena	Kwabana	Kwabena
Wednesday	Manlaa	Wukuada	Akua/Ahu	Akua	Kwaku	Kwaku
Thursday	Wuhué	Yawoada	Yaa/Aya	Yaa	Kwaw/Yaw	Yaw
Friday	Yaa	Fiada	Afua/Afué	Afua/Afia	Kofi	Kofi
Saturday	Fué	Memeneda	Ama/Amoa (nasal)	Ama	Kwame	Kwame
Sunday	Mɔlɛ	Kwasiada	Akwasi/ Akisi/ Akosua	Akosua	Kwasi	Kwasi

Among the Anyii, Akwasi is the equivalent of the female Sunday-born Akosua in Twi (pronounced with same tonality as in Akosua). The Anyii also name a Sunday-born girl child Akisi or Akosua. Kwaw is more common among the Anyii than Yaw for a Thursday-born male child.

There are female names like Kwasibala, Kwadwobala, and so on. *Balaa* (*ɔbaa* in Twi) is Anyii for "female. Therefore, Kwasi-bala and Kwadwo-bala, respectively translate as "Kwasi-ette" and "Kwadwo-ette," where a female child has been named after a male relative whose kra da or day name is Kwasi or Kwadwo. It is evident that among Anyii, kra da or day names are sometimes used as proper names. If the female child were to use her own day name, she would be Akosua/Akisi/Akwasi because she was born on a Sunday, and Adwa (Adwoa in Twi) because she was born on a Monday.

Death

Traditional Akan belief holds that the dead are still with the living. In other words, the dead live in an out-of-world community called Nwomee Kulo in Anyii and Nsamanfoɔ Kurom or Asamando in Twi, where none dies again. Nwomee Kulo or Asamando simply means "town of ghosts" or better yet, "land of the dead."

The belief system recognizes what some writers have called "the living dead," where the dead live in an outer world but within a comfortable reach of mortals. Hence, they are close enough to the living and quick enough to respond to invocations through libation and other calls and appeals for support, guidance, and protection from the machinations of evildoers among the living. When the Anyii say, "bɛ wu a, bɛ wɔ dɔ," which roughly translates as "the dead are still alive," they mean the dead are not far off and are aware of the material needs and spiritual support of those they have left behind.

Akan Twi-Fante love funerals, especially the Twi subgroup. Sometimes one gets the impression Akan Twi pray to have more funerals in order to show off the latest in red or black fashion design. It seems this last rite of passage that is supposed to be solemn has been turned into an occasion not very different from some hilarious, high-expectation event. This is not an exaggeration or a stereotypical observation. Funerals have evolved into a lucrative industry among Akan Twi-Fante. A few individuals and families have been bankrupted as a direct result of funeral expenditures. A few traditional authorities among Akan Twi-Fante have decreed a cap on how much an individual should spend on funerals. The fact people continue to be burdened with funeral expenses speaks to the success or failure of such decrees. The irony is that quite often the person whose life is being celebrated at a great cost did not receive much attention or love from the same extended family that is over heads and heels about his death. The late K. Gyasi, a famous Ghanaian highlife musician of all time, masterfully captured the contradiction in one of his songs:

"ɔmama sɛ mere bɛ wu a, me nnim" (I know not when a noble heart like me is going to die) …

"Mo mma me nwu ansa, na mo ahyehyɛ me sɛ ayeforɔ" (It's of no use giving me a royal treatment upon death; dressing up my corpse as if I was a bride on her wedding day.)

"Onipa wu a, na wa nya asɛɛ" (Because a dead person is a lost asset) …

"ɛda a, m'awu da hɔ no, ɛhɔ na obi bɛ hunu sɛ me wɔ abusuafoɔ" (The day I die, many strangers are they who will present themselves as family mourning me) …

"Abusuapanin afira kuntunkuni, ɔ de biribi abɔ ne ti … afei wa kɔ tena kaa front …" (Someone will spot head of my family sitting in the front passenger seat of a bus, all decked up in the most expensive funeral attire) …

"ɛhɔ na obi bɛ bisa no sɛɛ: W ɔfa Kwasi na wo re kɔ he ni? ..." (Whereupon someone will ask: where to, Uncle Kwasi?) ...

"ɔse m'ani abere ..." ("It's a hard day today. I'm grieving the death of my beloved nephew," he will reply) ...

"Me ara me re si mu akɔ Kumase akɔ tɔ fun-nakaa ... (And I am travelling to Kumase to purchase his coffin. I'm not leaving the role to anybody because my late nephew meant so much to me) ...

"Me wɔ nkwa mu yi deɛ, sɛ mo wɔ mmoa bi a, momfa moa me" (I entreat my family to care about my welfare while I'm alive; and not to defer their love and assistance until after my death, when it will mean nothing to me.)

"ɔmama sɛ mere bɛ wu a, me nnim" (I know not when a noble heart like me is going to die) ...

Beside the commercial aspect of it, funerals are one occasion at which the finest in Akan culture is put on display. From elaborate rites to drumming and dance, the celebration is a veritable exhibition of authentic culture by the most eloquent, knowledgeable, and versatile. And if the funeral is for a person of high royalty, say a chief or king, the history of the people stretching back in time will be relived. In this case, the celebration will typically trace back to the original home of the community or people, victories in war, alliances in times of war and national difficulties, and collective achievements. The historical accounts will often be told in a combination of proverbial oratory, talking drum language, songs (especially war songs), and in gestured pantomime.

Another item on the list of mourning the dead among the Akan is the dirge. A dirge is an art form in which a raconteur extols the virtues of an individual during his lifetime. The format is set between weeping and storytelling, in a mournful rendition of a noble background and a life well lived. Dirges are exclusively the domain of women who must have a profound knowledge of the subject's roots or family history and above-average eloquence in presenting that knowledge amid tearful sobs. The most skillful among dirge raconteurs are often available for hire to grace funerals of important members of society.

Funerals among Akan are also occasions for reunion, when families far and wide come home to bid a loved one the last rite of passage. It is not uncommon for a family to keep the body of a dead relative at the morgue in order to allow relatives from around the world return home to participate in the final rite of passage. It is also part of Akan culture that funeral donations and contributions (*nsaa* in Twi; *nzaa* in Anyii) are a collective effort, usually presented in the name of the children, siblings or in-laws of the dearly departed. As for surviving members of the abusua, custom expects them to take responsibility for all funeral costs and residual debts.

Typical Akan funeral clothing is red or black, sewn from plain cotton material or the rich-textured, high-end type called *kuntunkuni*. The exception is when white clothing is worn to celebrate the life of a patriarch or matriarch. White is the symbol of happiness or victory, while red and black is for painful moments and mourning.

Until the recent past, the first level family members, such as siblings, children, nephews, nieces, and sometimes grandchildren, would be required to shave off their hair as part of the mourning process, if the departed was a matriarch or a patriarch. The shaving of hair is usually accompanied by a few days of fasting, a symbolic gesture of the painful loss of a beloved family member. Akan Anyii-Baulé call it *kyi sεε* (literally, funeral self-denial) or *abuada*, as is also known among Akan Twi-Fante. Regarding widows, they would be required to shave off their hair as well as spend forty days in seclusion (not isolation) and in mourning cloth (red or black) from the day of the death of their husbands. They may not engage in any work activity beyond basic personal domestic chores. During the forty-day seclusion period, they would be attended to by female members of their families as well as those of their late husbands' families. Observance of the forty-day seclusion is known among Akan Anyii-Baulé as *amgboti*; the same is *kunaa* among Akan Twi-Fante. Widowers do not shave off their hair or undergo the forty-day mourning rite.

Elaborate funerals are not performed for first-child deaths. By first-child death is meant a woman who has never lost a child until now. Akan Twi-Fante call the occurrence *sodeɛ* while Akan Anyii-Baulé call it *fɛ wa*, roughly translated as "sweet child." The belief is that a full service funeral for a sodeɛ or fɛ wa will give the wrong impression to the spirit of death that it had succeeded in causing great grief to the affected household, that it would spur it to take away the souls of more children from the same family. Therefore, the rite of passage is limited to a gathering of close relatives at the family house for a few hours only. Mourners, including the grieving mother, are discouraged from crying at the loss of a sodeɛ or fɛ wa child. The child in sodeɛ or fɛ wa is not measured in years. One could be a parent or even a grandparent, for as long as one becomes the first child to die, one satisfies the definition of sodeɛ or fɛ wa.

The Trouble with the "Returning Infant"

There is such a thing as a "returning infant" in Akan traditional belief. A returning infant is when a woman goes through a few deliveries, only for the child to die in infancy each time. It is believed a returning infant is only out to play on the vulnerability of a woman in need of a child, giving her emotional pain and sorrow where she needs happiness, joy, and maternal fulfillment.

When the local priest or other seer has concluded that a child is out to play pranks and deny a woman the joy of motherhood, a plan is hatched to put a stop to the revolving-door occurrence. A priest or an elder will be asked to make atypical tribal incisions into the face of a child believed to be a returning infant, a week or two following birth. Additionally, the child will be given a name considered unsavory or even insulting, like Kanga, Mosi, Aseawié/Aseayié (among Akan Anyii-Baulé), and Donkor, Mosi, Asaseasa (among Akan Twi-Fante). It is believed that the combined effects of facial mutilation and "bad name" assignment constitute sufficient humiliation to stop the returning baby from returning to the land of the dead and in the process, ensure happiness, contentment, and fulfilment to his poor mother. The Igbo of Nigeria call such a child an "ogbanjé".

εlε Soo Aleε—Calling Home the Living Dead

It is not about mute zombies dragging their weighty bodies about town, sometimes causing harm to the living. Nor is it about dry bone skeletons suddenly gathering themselves together and springing to life to terrorize the neighborhood in hollowed-out eye sockets and unprovoked, perpetual laughter. Rather, it is about a ceremony where the spirit of a dearly departed is specially invited to interact with the real world in real time. In this one-of-a-kind ceremony, the *nwomee* (Twi: *saman*) or ghost is invited to engage in a discourse with the living.

ɛlɛ Soo Aleɛ directly translates as "Meal of the Seventh Day." However, this is no ordinary meal, as its purpose and the description of its preparation will make clear.

The seventh day is actually one week less a day following the burial of a dead relative. The Anyii, like the other Akan groups, have an eight-day week (Anyii: ɛlɛbotwɛ; Twi: Nnawotwe) because counting, unlike in European culture, for example, includes the day of the present. This is the day when the funeral for the departed includes the special side offer of ɛlɛ Soo Aleɛ ritual, if the family believes the circumstances surrounding the person's death warrant clearing the air about some alleged foul play or unnatural cause. Though it is supposed to be a special meal on the seventh day, the ceremony, when it is performed, actually happens on the eighth day, which is the same as one week following the day of death, on the occasion of the observance of the one-week funeral. By the end of the ritual, those who believe in the truthfulness or utility of ɛlɛ Soo Aleɛ will have had closure and answers to some previously unresolved family or other issues and questions. ɛlɛ Soo Aleɛ is more a bundle than just a meal. But the central purpose and theme of the ritual is the summoning of the spirit of the deceased from the land of the dead, to come testify to the living and to do so in public.

There is no clear justification why the subject of ɛlɛ Soo Aleɛ is almost always a woman. Any attempt to answer the question remains a conjecture, at best. Be as it may, when the spirit that is invoked comes to life, spirits of other deceased members from the community also "call in," uninvited, as if to crash the party and engage the living in discourse. Though ɛlɛ Soo Aleɛ is typically a women affair, the uninvited spirits sometimes include male spirits or ghosts. They either directly possess someone from among the audience at the funeral or speak through the agency of the principal person at the center of the ɛlɛ Soo Aleɛ ceremony. Some of these spirits bear greetings and messages from one or other long-deceased family member.

Very early the morning of the seventh day, and before people gather for the seventh-day funeral, elderly women of the clan meet at the burial grounds of the deceased relative whose spirit they intend to invite to engage the community. There they prepare a bundle that will later be placed on the head of a designated young woman; a virgin is preferred. The contents of the bundle will include the deceased's favorite dish when she was alive, a piece of her favorite clothing, and just about anything she left behind that was near and dear to her when she was among the living. The location to set up and prepare the spirit or ghost can equally be at the edge of town, away from human or other traffic and interruption.

Once prepared, the bundle of εlε Soo Aleε is placed on the head of the chosen young woman. The leader of the group will then call the spirit of the dead, reciting special incantations handed down by generations, until the spirit or ghost takes possession of the body of the young woman carrying the bundle. In a trancelike state, the possessed young woman begins to speak in a voice similar to the deceased's when she was alive and even assumes her recognized gait and other body language features. When the spirit has fully possessed the carrier, the party heads toward the funeral grounds, which, by this time, is filled to capacity. Upon arrival, all eyes and attention are focused on the young woman possessed with the spirit of the deceased, in anticipation of the message she has brought from Bɔlε (Twi: Asamando) or the land of the dead.

Subject matter can range from the mundane and general to the serious and specific; from the personal to the communal; from an admission of guilt to the denial of same; from accusations and threats to an apology; from a state of belligerence to an appeal for peace; or the spirit in residence will come bearing greetings from ancestors from the land of the dead and an admonition to the living to close ranks and love one another. Sometimes she will join in dance with the living at her own funeral, a few final steps of nostalgia, never able to repeat again.

After she has delivered her message and perhaps danced a lap, the spirit will bid farewell to all gathered and depart from the funeral grounds toward the edge of town, as her handlers follow the young woman bearing the bundle on her head. There, the ladies who prepared the εlε Soo Aleε will disassemble the bundle and free and disengage the carrier young lady from the spirit world, who will then reclaim herself and return to the land of the living, where she properly belongs.

Aside from εlε Soo Aleε, there are instances when the ghost of the dead is said to have descended on somebody. This phenomenon may happen when the dead body is being conveyed to the cemetery for burial, or at a later day at the funeral grounds, but more on the day of the burial. The Anyii refer to such a happening as *nwomee agua ye* (the ghost has descended upon him/her), as distinct from εlε Soo Aleε where, typically, the occurrence is a planned, deliberate call-up. The key difference between εlε Soo Aleε and nwomee agua ye is that while there is an element of inducement in the former, the latter phenomenon is involuntary and spontaneous. In the case of nwomee agua ye, it is the ghost of the dead that itches to say something, uninvited and unprovoked. On almost all occasions, the subject matter is either about pleading guilt or innocence about something he or she was suspected to have done while among the living. Another distinguishing element of nwomee agua ye is that the phenomenon is not limited to deceased women only. Again, while εlε Soo Aleε is a planned ceremony, nwomee agua ye is unplanned and not ceremonial. Both happenings, however, share in the common characteristic that they happen at burial or funeral grounds.

Indeed, "bɛ wu a, bɛ wɔ dɔ" (the dead are alive somewhere) is a common refrain among the Anyii.

Inheritance

This section assumes traditional inheritance among Anyii and also other Akan groups. Typically, traditional inheritance is intestate and derives usage and interpretation from the matrilineal Akan system. The discussion excludes inheritance to the royal stool, which has been covered in another section of this book.

In old Anyii and Akan societies, widows and their children were generally left out of a man's estate, unless he had designated landed property and other assets to his spouse and children when he was alive. The reason behind this cultural behavior was that by way of children born to his wife, the deceased has bequeathed greater wealth to the woman and her extended family than landed property he is leaving behind. A section in this book discussed traditional Akan worldview of family and lineage and touched on the subject of children belonging to the family of the female spouse as well as the cultural view that a breathing human being is many times worthier than landed property and other asset acquisitions. Based on this interpretation, Anyii and other Akan hold the view that a widow has already been compensated from a man's estate, and handsomely so. However, a widow so treated will be allowed use and ownership of some family asset—for example, a piece of land to farm on. Nevertheless, she and her children are excluded from the direct and full ownership of the property of their late husband and father.

An element of intestate inheritance is that the man inherited or farmed on family property he was entrusted with and should, therefore, not pass it on to his widow or children who, by traditional Akan definition, belong to another family. If the deceased left behind a last will and testament in which he signed off property he had inherited from his traditional family, it is very likely members of the extended family will mount a legal challenge to his distributed estate on the grounds the family property was an inheritance in trust that did not warrant passing it on outside the matrilineal family line. Urbanization, education, and the money economy have all positively changed people's perceptions and attitude to the general question of inheritance where property in trust is at stake. In our times, the modern state has sought a balance between traditional practices and statutory law.

Among the Anyii, the property of a female who dies intestate is inherited by her children, almost always by her daughters. Traditional Anyii and Akan society does not speak highly of a male dependent on a woman, especially in marriage. The same thought process seems to be extended to inheritance.

Awobaa

The Anyii call it "Awobaa." The same is "Awowa" in Twi. Awobaa or Awowa is a contractual work relationship that comes into force when a debtor has failed to meet an obligation to a creditor. The practice is not slavery; there is no element of ownership, coercion, or free labor. It is not bondage, because one under the conditions of Awobaa continues to enjoy his liberty and freedom as before. Awobaa has time limits, itself agreed upon between creditor and debtor, to the value of a predetermined amount owing. There was hardly abuse of the person serving under Awobaa because, in most cases, the lender was from the same community or the next town. People were so closely connected that hardly would a lender come from abroad or take undue advantage of the Awobaa system without repercussions.

When a borrower has failed to settle a debt, he may offer his creditor the option to go work for him for a specified length of time as payment in kind for money owed. Length of time may range from a few months to a couple of years and is based on an estimated value of debt owed. If married, the household of one under Awobaa would be excluded from the labor contract. If creditor and debtor lived in the same town, the one serving Awobaa could spend some days of the week to tend to his own farm in order to feed his family. Sometimes a relative will perform Awobaa duties on behalf of the delinquent borrower. This last fact manifests the depth of commitment members of traditional Anyii or Akan family have toward one another, as a result of what is one's business is every family member's business.

Chapter 12

Festivals, Rites, and Rituals

Eluedie (Yam Festival)

The annual yam festival is arguably the most important event on the traditional calendars of Akan Anyii-Baulé. *Elué* is yam among Anyii-Baulé tribes. To Anyii-Baulé, the tuber of this climber plant is the prize produce of all food crops. There are varieties of yams, among them *kpona* (*pona* in Twi), *asɔbayerɛ*, *nzaa*, and *gbodoo* (water yam). There is *bolué*, short for *bolo élué*, or wild yam—wild because it is not domesticated or cultivated. In Akan Twi-Fante, bolué is *aha bayerɛ*. There is also *kokoase élué* among Anyii-Baulé, and *kokoase bayerɛ* among Akan Twi-Fante. This specie thrives best in cocoa farms, hence the reference to cocoa in "kokoase." Up to this point, it must be obvious to the reader that *bayerɛ* is Akan Twi-Fante for yam. But the *éluédié* or *éluélié* yam festival celebrates kpona, the recognized king among yams, and to some extent, the *nzaa* specie.

Eluedié or éluélié roughly translates as "celebration of yam" or "yam festival." The importance of éluédié is not so much the fact it happens about the same time every year (in late May or early June) and is therefore predictable but that the event celebrates abundance as a direct result of the community's hard work and industry. Farming is the main economic activity among Akan Anyii-Baulé, and eluedie is the celebration of the first fruit of the season. To that end, éluédié is thanksgiving of sorts.

Beside the gastronomical aspect of it, éluédié assesses the spiritual situation of the community for the year just ended and seeks blessings for the present and future. The festival is an elaborate display of the rich culture of the people, where the chief or king sits in state to receive homage and preside over proceedings. The proceedings include the best in cultural pageantry, especially among young women. The *kɔmea* (*kɔmfo* in Twi) or state fetish priest, assisted by less notable ones, plays key roles in the spiritual well-being of the nation and is therefore central to the éluédié festival. In recent times, however, leaders of monotheistic religions have taken up roles in the spiritual aspect of éluédié festivities.

For Anyii Dwabene, éluédié happens after celebration by Abron Bonduku. As I have stated elsewhere in this book, the former opted deference to the latter when liberating warriors from Dadieso eventually accepted an offer to settle on Abron Bonduku land. In recognition of Abron as original landlord, Dwabene gave deference without prompting or coercion and certainly not as a vassal state to the former. By offering the Anyii Dwabene free land to settle on, the Abron not only showed gratitude to their liberators but more importantly as a protective insurance against possible future attack by their Bouna or other traditional enemies. Anyii Dwabene as a next-door neighbor was good politics for Abron Bonduku. The fraternal arrangement dates back to the very founding of Anyii Dwabene state in 1750.

Ndɛɛ

While none prays for death to lay its icy hands on anybody, especially, a close and well-loved relative, Anyii culture celebrates the death of the very old. The funeral for a centenarian or someone around that age bracket includes an elaborate ceremony called Ndɛɛ.

Ndɛɛ is Anyii for elephant grass. The ceremony is so called because it involves young adults, children, and indeed any second or subsequent generation descendant of the deceased stomping the ground with cut stems of elephant grass as they parade through the main streets of the town. The parade and stomping are accompanied by special-purpose songs for the occasion.

Celebrants dress in simple garments. The girls wrap a one-piece cloth covering up to the lower neckline. For the boys, a simple shirt or singlet over a pair of shorts is common dress code. The faces, shoulders, and neck areas of celebrants are decorated with white ochre patterns. Among the Akan and also among several other African ethnic groups, applying white ochre to the body indicates victory, joy, or celebration. Similarly, red ochre often symbolizes sorrow and sadness. The same Akan worldview applies in the wearing of white cloths to symbolize celebration or victory, and red or black in times of sadness and sorrow.

Typical Ndɛɛ songs deride, taunt, and mourn the deceased in equal measure. Ndɛɛ celebrates women, often considered matriarchs, who pass on at an advanced age, as the following song testifies:

Akɔ taa awu oo

Wa ma ye mma mmɔ ba yɛ wanzo

Translation: "Mother hen is dead, leaving her chicks distraught and in disarray."

Another popular Ndɛɛ song emphasizing age and perceived resistance to death goes like this:

Eee, Nana nwa wɔ nwu ma ooo!

Wa wu afoɔ he ooo!

"Nana (dear old lady) has been resisting death, but couldn't this time around!"

Ndɛɛ is celebrated as part of the fortieth-day funeral ceremony, or an appointed day in lieu. In typical Akan culture, a funeral is a death event separate from a burial. In other words, funerals are held on a day in the future after the burial. The time lapse allows the community and especially families to properly organize themselves to say a fitting and final farewell to a dearly departed. There is the seventh-day funeral, which is more a gathering of the family to plan the main funeral on the fortieth day after death.

The fortieth day is significant because in the Akan belief system, the soul of a dead person continues to lurk around the living until after performance of the fortieth-day funeral, when it will leave definitively for the land of the ancestors. Therefore, in typical Akan belief, the newly dead would be left meals every night in a designated corner of the house until after the final funeral rites. It is further believed that where a fortieth-day funeral has not been performed for whatever reason, the soul becomes unsettled and a vagrant, alternating between the world of mortals and the netherworld. The name for such in Akan Twi-Fante is *saman twɛn-twɛn* (literally, a "waiting ghost"). When it is believed there is a saman twɛn-twɛn, the community performs a special ceremony to bid a proper farewell to the soul of the deceased. There is also the one-year funeral, which is more a memorial and a gathering of the extended family. Properly speaking, there is no customary requirement to hold a one-year funeral.

The Ndɛɛ celebrants end up at the funeral grounds where, since early in the day, the entire community and others from out of town have gathered to pay last respects to the deceased.

Nzuénu

Anyii culture celebrates a rite of passage for girls into womanhood. There is no similar rite of passage for boys, however. The specific custom is called Nzuénu, which roughly translates as the "Water-Dipping Ceremony." Nzué is water in Anyii. Part of the Nzuénu ceremony involves taking the young woman to a specially designated stream for a ritual bath. Nzuénu is a puberty rite, the outdooring by the community of a young woman transitioning from girlhood into womanhood, whose hand may be asked for in marriage.

A young woman undergoing the Nzuénu process is called an Atɔmvɔlɛ, as distinct from a Konya, which is Anyii for bride. The name differentiation underscores the fact that though Anyii culture outdoors a young woman as eligible for marriage, that fact alone is not enough reason to encumber or pressure a young woman into marriage. In other words, though there is evidence of arranged marriage among the Anyii, forced marriage is not a cultural practice. Nor is it morally acceptable. Young women have the freedom to marry now or in the future, and to whomever they wish.

When a family becomes aware their young daughter has started menstruating, they prepare themselves to perform the Nzuénu ceremony. Family in this context means the womenfolk from either side of the girl's parents' extended family. Strictly speaking, Anyii custom requires the performance of Nzuénu on a young woman, without which a man seen with her in an uncompromising way would be deemed a child molester. Also, Nzuénu is a way of informing the community and especially prospective suitors that the hand of the young woman may be asked for in marriage. As expected, Nzuénu is a strictly women affair.

Some observers and commentators refer to Nzuénu as Kodjo. This is inaccurate. Kodjo quite simply is the ensemble of ritual dress that a young lady assumes during Nzuénu ceremony. While there is such a statement in Anyii as "Ba to ye Nzuénu" (literally, "She has undergone the Nzuénu ritual'), it is not proper statement to say, for example, that "Ba to ye Kodjo," or "Ba fité ye Kodjo" ("She has undergone or been outdoored Kodjo"'). Therefore, while Kodjo is part of Nzuénu, the reverse cannot be true. Kodjo is a subset of Nzuénu; it is the costume of Nzuénu.

Kodjo is the ensemble of traditional female underwear or loincloth known to the Anyii as *asiaa*, which is held together by waist beads. In Akan

Twi-Fante, asiaa is the same as *tam* or *amoaseɛ*. The difference between everyday asiaa and kodjo is that while the former is compact, the latter is overflowing in size and spread. Also, kodjo is worn by young women for the Nzuénu ceremony and by fetish priest assistants on occasions such as the annual éluédié or yam festival. In sum, Kodjo is a special-purpose female loincloth or underwear.

The asiaa is passed between the upper thighs of the atɔmvɔlɛ and tucked in between waist beads and the skin just below the navel and above the buttocks. For the occasion of Nzuénu and for good measure, the extra piece of asiaa is distributed evenly in front and behind the atɔmvɔlɛ, usually up to the knee, offering extra coverage and security, because unlike standard dress-up asiaa, which is a covered undergarment, kodjo is an outwear.

On the day of Nzuénu, the atɔmvɔlɛ is well coiffured, manicured, and rubbed in shea butter oil. She is decorated with expensive beads around her wrists, ankles, and neck and extending over a pair of full, firm breasts. The reflection of the sun on her smooth, gleaming dark skin gives the atɔmvɔlɛ an aura of a goddess. On Nzuénu day, an atɔmvɔlɛ is treated like royalty. She does not perform any chores and is provided with everything necessary for her comfort and the occasion. She has assistants and servants at her beck and call. Nzuénu is usually rounded off with girl games, like *ampé*, that run late into the night.

The Nzuénu ceremony comes with its own

special dish. Among the Anyii, the favorite dish for an atɔmvɔlɛ is mashed yam served with palm oil and topped with boiled eggs. This is a popular dish among the Akan, known as *ɛtɔ* or *mvufu*. Sometimes communities celebrate young women of atɔmvɔlɛ age in group Nzuénu ceremonies. For the young women, not only is the celebration a rite of passage, but the collective event creates a bond among them and becomes a point of reference that gets etched in memory well into old age.

Mumumé

Mumumé is a secret ritual performed by adult women. It involves women stripped to their traditional asiaa (Twi: tam or amoaseɛ) underwear. The asiaa is a strip of special-purpose cotton wear, usually red in color, that is passed between the upper thighs to cover a woman's private part. The asiaa is then knotted in two places—in front just below the navel and behind the wearer's back, above the buttocks, to elaborate waist beads to hold it in place. The women all go topless in a Mumumé ritual.

The village or town is notified when a Mumumé is going to take place. The village or town gets locked down on the assigned day. It is believed that if an adult male deliberately spies on a Mumumé procession, he will become impotent or, even worse, go mad.

The belief behind Mumumé is that strange and unusual events or occurrences are the machinations of evil spirits. For example, an epidemic, eclipse, or some unexplained mysterious disease or phenomenon is believed to have been caused by one or other evil spirit. To adherents, evil must be expelled with a ritual like Mumumé; otherwise the affliction will remain with the community. Mumumé, therefore, is a protest ritual to hoot at and thereby expel evil spirits believed to have invaded the community on a mission of harm and destruction. Mumumé intends to ward off evil and protect the community.

Women in Mumumé mode walk back and forth the length of the town's main street, chanting war songs. No musical instruments accompany the war songs in a Mumumé procession. At intervals and in unison, the women all bend over in one direction, as if to expose their private parts to the invading evil spirits who, it is believed, take flight at feminine nudity.

A Mumumé ritual lasts only a few hours of a day and happens perhaps once in a generation. Among the Anyii, the ritual is one avenue to expel evil and fear as well as release stress, tension, and uncertainty about the unknown. The belief assures psychological safety and equilibrium, even if it does not stand up to scientific or logical scrutiny to most. But to the extent that it relieves fear and psychological discomfort, Mumumé has an emotional attachment and utility to those who believe in it.

In the worldview of traditional society where scientific inquiry has little value, the world is peopled by spirits—some good, others bad. Most social problems are believed to have spiritual sponsors who must be engaged and, in some cases, neutralized through the medium of the spirit world and the intervention of those believed to have four eyes—namely voyeurs. In this context, Mumumé and similar beliefs have played useful roles in traditional nation building, crisis management, and group psychology.

Chapter 13

The Anyii at Play

Song and Dance

When they decide to wind down, so to speak, after a hard day's work, the Anyii say, "amɔ ma yɛ hɔ ha ngɔhoa" (Twi: "mo ma yɛnkɔ goro"), meaning "let us go play." Ngɔhoa in Anyii means a game or play, and the best setting is under a moonlit night, after a hard day's work of farming activity. Those were the days when everything went natural, including night vision.

The Kotoko emigrants who founded Nkrankwanta brought with them traditional dances different from the cultural repertoire of their non-Anyii neighbors across the border in Ngyeresa or the Gold Coast. Famous among these dances are Abodaa, Ndolua, Mbɛlɛ, Alatoo, and a few others. Abodaa is the main dance type among all Anyii subgroups and is sometimes called Asamane. While drumming for all other dance types is done by beating the surface of the drums, drumming for Mbɛlɛ is done by hitting the outer frame of the hollowed-out wooden drum.

It is instructive to mention that Akan Anyii-Baulé tribes, though all migrated from south-central Ghana, do not dance Adowa, the popular dance form familiar with most Akan Twi-Fante tribes. It is therefore reasonable to conclude that as a dance form, Adowa evolved after the migration of Akan Anyii-Baulé tribes. It is also reasonable to say that for a considerable length of time, there was minimal official contact and, if at all, a weak link between Anyii-Baulé groups and their respective former homes in Ghana, else they would have collectively shared in the evolution of Adowa with their Twi-speaking cousins. However, the Anyii share with Akan Twi-Fante most royal courts and what may be called sacred drumming and dance forms. Sacred, because the big drums and accompanying royal dances are reserved for special and rare occasions, such as the funeral of a departed chief or king or as part of the coronation ceremony of a new one. The dance types include Mbindini (Mpintin in Twi), Kyenea/Kenea Pili (Twene Kɛseɛ in Twi), literally "big drums" (Fontromfrom among Akan Twi-Fante), and a few others. Again, the inference is that the shared dance forms predate migration of Anyii-Baulé groups from south-central Ghana.

Of dancing to Kyenea/Kenea Pili, it is generally believed among Anyii-Baulé tribes that one requires four eyes in order to safely navigate or maneuver the open court solo dance to the sacred drums. To have four eyes is another way of saying one must have spiritual powers. Kyenea/Kenea Pili is a drumming and dancing session only; there is no song accompaniment. The occasion for a session is so rare it can take as much as a whole generation for one to witness a Kyenea/Kenea Pili drumming and dance.

An Anyii fluent in Twi and sufficiently versed in proverbs and the language of the talking drums better understands and appreciates classical Asante culture than the average Asante. The reason is that much of the root words, expressions, and general structure of the proverbs and tunes of the talking drums are in old Asante, which is probably closer to Anyii than to contemporary Asante Twi. Indeed, the elderly often remind that Asante Twi as a language has redefined itself from what it was a few decades ago. Language as part of cultural evolution is a fact in human history, in time and place. For the Anyii-Baoulé group, cultural evolution has been as a result of migration from their original homes in south-central Ghana and the influences of neighbors in their respective new environments. This is not to mention the controlling influence of different and often competing European colonial powers. While the tribes of Akan Twi-Fante were almost entirely colonized by imperial Britain, much of Akan Anyii-Baulé fell under the less culture-friendly republicanism of French colonial rule.

Abodaa is the main dance of the Anyii. Dancers are usually in pairs of a man and a woman, who respond to the call of the *atumgbala* (Twi: *atumpan*) talking drums. To the uninitiated, the beauty and wonder of Abodaa lie in the near perfect timing of when dancers change steps, rise, or get down to business, so to speak, on the dance floor. The lock-step unison in dance moves is captivating. But all that the dancers are doing is responding to the instructions of the atumgbala.

Comparative male-female Abodaa dance poses.
The female is slightly bent with an outstretched,
downward open left palm. The male dancer,
also slightly bent, does not open the palm and
dances with both hands closer to the body.

Four dancers demonstrate more clearly the female dance pose of Abodaa. In this photo, the dancers appear to be in a file, but dancing in file formation is not typical of Abodaa.

It is debatable, but the Anyii Sanvi, whose territory borders the Nzema to the south and close to the Gulf of Guinea, believe they are an authority on the best in Anyii art form, especially in regards to dance and music. Could the assertion be related to the stereotype that communities that live close to or along seashores have relatively more time on their hands to indulge in partying and entertainment, generally?

The atumgbala is a pair of long, hollowed-out tree trunks covered on one end with treated antelope or duiker hide that is strung taut over the surface. The drummer sits behind the raised atumgbala and beats it with special purpose sticks. Other drums, called *kyene nzini* (Twi: *twene sini*; literally, short drums), smaller and single in assemblage, held in an upright position (usually between the drummer's open thighs) and beaten with open palms, accompany the cacophony of the orchestral ensemble. In all Abodaa sessions, the atumgbala player acts as musical conductor who initiates the next piece and signals its end.

The atumgbala drums are not a set of primary talking drums, yet they "talk" during Abodaa session. They assume a talking role insofar as they call out nicknames or a pet, streetwise expression of a dancer who has taken to the dance floor. The appellation is often intended to acknowledge the presence of an important person or bolster the ego of a neighborhood popular guy. A typical talking drum among the Akan is a set of dedicated drums whose use and utility is more for transmitting messages than for dance and general entertainment. Talking drums are typically shorter and wider than atumgbala.

Abodaa drumming and dance is accompanied by singing, usually about everyday social issues and often expressed in proverbs or popular say-say. The women begin the chorus, and the men respond in like manner, repeating same lyrics or sometimes embellishing the statement in the lyrics initiated by the female singers. The female singers clap along the song at the same time. One popular Abodaa song philosophizes:

> Kyanamaa te nzu? (What good is beauty?)

> Kyanamaa te bɛ nwo yalɛ. (Beauty is sometimes a curse.)

Another Abodaa song very popular with Anyii Dwabene is tongue in cheek about someone who breaks a rule or taboo, knowing very well he will ultimately pay for the consequences:

> Wa yɔ bɔ bɛ nyɔ ma oo, ooo

> Na mma bɛ yɔ oo, ooo, oo

> Wa yɔ bɔ bɛ nyɔ ma oo, ooo

But before an Abodaa session seriously gets under way or thickens, so to speak, there is this opening song, whose obvious intent is to invite or rally the community to participate in the dancing event at hand:

Bɛ yia oo,

Bea mmɔ, bɛ yia oo, ooo ...

Roughly translated, the opening song means: "Gather, people gather ..."

In between breaks and often as a prelude and an introduction to the next tune, a call-and-answer vocal piece accompanied by a casual note on a lone *kyene nzini* drum takes place. The piece, unlike the main Abodaa song that immediately follows it, is a choral display among male singers. A lead raconteur initiates a call, and the others either chorus in or respond with a well-known answer. The lyrics vary in subject matter but are often in praise of some important person or about some major event in the past.

The popular name is *pɛ di* (Twi: *twa di*), literally, "say something" session. Pɛ di can be likened to an acappella session. A very popular pɛ di among Anyii Dwabene is in praise of Nana Kwaw Bilé, the longest-ruling Dwabene king in recent memory (1934–82), and goes like this:

Akosua ma me nna ase ooo

Akosua ma me nna ase ooo

Akosua ma me nna ase

Eéé, bɛ kɔ a, bɛ sé Nana Kwaw Bilé me da ye ase ooo

Akosua ma me nna ase ooo

Akosua ma me nna ase

In rough translation:

I must give thanks. (Three times.)

Somebody tell Nana Kwaw Bilé that I thank him.

I must give thanks.

In place of Nana Kwaw Bilé, another chief's or high royal's name is sometimes inserted.

Unlike Abodaa, Ndolua, or the other Anyii dances, Alatoo is usually danced at night, and in the olden days when few towns had electricity, under the glare of the full moon. Also, Alatoo is more a dance of Anyii Bini. Not all Anyii subgroups have Alatoo in their repertoire of traditional dances.

In addition to the old and what may be called root dances, such as Abodaa, Ndolua, and Kyenea/ Kenea Pili, the ever-innovative and resourceful Anyii have developed other dance genres over the years. We may classify these additions as new or contemporary. Of these, perhaps the three most popular are Sida, Adade, and Anoanzɛɛ, with the name of the last dance translating as Koroyɛ in Twi, or "Unity." Of the three, Sida is the most popular with Nkrankwanta.

Sida, Adade, and Anoanzɛɛ are marching band type dances. Though not a brass band, horns accompany percussion and group singing. Dancers usually dress in uniform and march in two straight files. The orchestral arrangement is the alternation between song, horn, and drum sessions. A lead singer calls the tune, and the other singers join in; then the singers give way to the horn blowers to belt it out, usually in rhythmic rephrasing of the spoken-word song. As for the drums, they're the typical marching band type, strung over the drummer's shoulders, of different sizes and bellow. The lead horn player and drummer are, from time to time, and in turn, allowed a refrain in order to demonstrate their respective skills.

One song so popular among all the Anyii groups

seems to be the central nervous system and very reason Sida, Adade, and Anoanzɛɛ were invented:

> Ewué bɔ me wu nyɛ me ya ééé …

> Ewué bɔ me wu nyɛ me ya ééé,
> Nana Ama

> Bafa nnɛteɛ agua me so oo,
> aééé …

> Literally: "Nana Ama, my death does not bother me so much as the fact I will be covered with earth."

Among the Akan, it is an endearment and a sign of respect to address someone "Nana." Nana is an honorific often reserved for kings, chiefs, and grandparents. Therefore, to address someone "Nana" is to accord great respect to that person. The song above is a lamentation to Nana Ama about a fact of life.

A Sida session at Nkrankwanta would be considered incomplete until the following has been sung:

> Akonyima Damoa ééé

> Wɔni wa bɔ wɔ ne wɔ di

Yeɛ wɔ ku wɔ ooo

Eéé Damoa ééé, ééé

Wɔni wa bɔ wɔ ne wɔ di

Yeɛ wɔ ku wɔ ooo

The song reminds the cockerel (Anyii: *akɔ nyima*; Twi: *akokɔnini*), whose traditional nickname is Damoa, that his worst enemy is from among his siblings. There is a saying in Akan Twi-Fante with the same import: "Aboa bi bɛ ka wo a, efiri wo ntoma mu"; literally, "An insect bite is more likely from within your garment than from without." Similarly, here are the lyrics of one of the songs of Bob Marley, the great reggae musician:

"Your worst enemy can be your best friend.

"And your best friend, your worst enemy …"

So though Anyii Kotoko left a great deal of memories behind at Kotokoso, they nevertheless brought with them the foundations of a new society not much different from what they had left behind. As for Kotokoso, the inhabitants of Awiasué, a neighboring Anyii Dwabene community, moved into the bigger and abandoned town, which continues to bear the same name. Kotokoso is a few miles across the border in Cote d'Ivoire, from Nkrankwanta.

Contemporary Music

In contemporary dance music, Akan Anyii-Baulé are less known than their Akan Twi-Fante cousins across the international frontier in Ghana. Perhaps it is because the popular highlife music that is almost synonymous with Ghana evolved in English-speaking West Africa to the exclusion of the French colonies, including Cote d'Ivoire, where most Akan Anyii-Baulé live. From the first recognized highlife recording in Ghana in 1928, which was a love song extoling the beauty of Yaa Amponsah, and of the same title, the immediate pre- and postindependence era produced some of the greatest traditional highlife music artistes in Ghana and West Africa. Great musicians like E.T. Mensah, Kakaiku, E.K. Nyame, Jerry Hansen, Nana Kwame Ampadu, and Amakye Dede have been popular with Akan Twi-Fante in Ghana as well as Akan Anyii-Baulé in Cote d'Ivoire.

But the music of Nana Kwame Ampadu holds a special place in the hearts of the immediate generation of post-independence Cote d'Ivoire. Perhaps it is because Kwame Ampadu and his African Brothers International Band toured and did shows in Cote d'Ivoire more than any of their competing contemporaries. But there is no doubt that as lead composer and singer, Kwame Ampadu's deep knowledge of Akan history and traditions, coupled with unmatched eloquence and style of delivery, has won him and his group more fans among Anyii-Baulé than any other highlife musician of his time.

"Kofi Nkrabea" and "Yaw Berko," a couple of the group's most successful songs, touch the sensibilities of almost every young Anyii-Baulé lover of highlife music. The narratives in both "Kofi Nkrabea" and "Yaw Berko" are the travails of two young men whose very names "Nkrabea" and "Berko," which translate as "Destiny" and "Born to Struggle," respectively, spell bad luck from the day each was born. It is obvious the song has resonated well with many Anyii-Baulé young men fighting uphill battles in life.

But Akan Anyii-Baulé has not been devoid of talent in popular music. Among the trailblazers were Les Soeurs Comoe (the Comoe Sisters), a sister-sister duo whose renditions not only touched on the issues of the day but also on the rights of women. In their "Adja me dédé ..." release in the early 1960s, Les Soeurs Comoe at once exposed and lamented the inhumanity and cruelty about a man who toiled and suffered in poverty with a wife only to divorce her, and without rights to property they had both acquired during the marriage, for a younger woman who would reap where she had not sowed. But the group hit the top of the charts with their "Abidjan pon so" release, a song celebrating the completion of the grand project of a major bridge across the Ebrié Lagoon in Abidjan, first capital city of Cote d'Ivoire.

Anoman Brou Félix and N'douba Kadjo were contemporaries of Les Soeurs Comoe. Later big-name Anyii-Baulé musicians include Eba Aka Jérome, a highlife artist, and Antoinette Konan. In Antoinette Konan, the audience is treated to a powerful rendition of traditional Baulé songs arranged in the best of modern acoustics and percussions and delivered in a voice as rich and controlled as the culture it showcases. "Abidjan Dja" is one compelling piece Ms. Konan will forever be remembered for.

Across the international border in Ghana, Francis Kenya (a.k.a. F. Kenya) stands tall among early traditional highlife musicians of all time. Most of his followers did not have to understand the lyrics of F. Kenya's music in the Nzema language in order to love the artist and his work. One popular piece, "awiéleε, dangama awiéleε, biala nze," reminds about the eternal truth that one knows not how one's last days on earth will look.

Among contemporary Anyii-Baulé musicians, perhaps Frédéric Désiré Ehui is the most successful and well known internationally. With the stage name Meiway, Frédéric has won several national and international musical awards, including as a four-time winner at the continental KORA All Africa Music Awards (the KORA Awards). The KORA Awards is the African equivalent of the American Grammy Awards.

Ngoaa or Stories (a.k.a. Kwaku Ananse Stories)

The Anyii-Baule, like their Twi-Fante cousins

across the border in Ghana, entertain with what is universally known as Kwaku Ananse stories. The general name of this form of entertainment is Ngoaa (Twi-Fante: Anansesɛm), in which Kyɛndaa (Ananse, in Twi-Fante), the proverbial wise, witty, and wily spider, plays a central character role.

The traditional setting of Ananse stories is around the fire in the early night, after the last meal. In an open-floor format, each person, young and old, narrates what he or she has heard told somewhere about some new Kwaku Ananse exploit or escapade. Beside its entertainment value, each Ngoaa or Anansesɛm ends with a lesson in morality.

There are also stories that entertain as well as pick the brain, as for example this one I remember told by my late uncle Kwadwo Tomea (Abdullah, following his conversion to Islam). It is a riddle that asks for listener input at the end of the narration.

There was this young man who lived with the parents on a farm. He was in an amorous but secretly kept relationship with a young woman who lived with her widower father on another farm. The two had marriage plans, but since the young man had not yet the means to support a family and therefore could not approach his lover's relatives with a proposal to marry their daughter, the relationship was being kept in secrecy. The two would get together in the dead of night, when everyone suspected they were asleep in their respective villages.

One very dark night, the young man visited his girlfriend on her father's farm. It was a practice that the young lady would keep her door unlocked each time she expected her lover's nocturnal visit. This would avoid a knock that might awaken or alert her father sleeping next-door. One late night, the young man visited his lover and, as usual, found her door unlocked. He entered and proceeded to engage in touching and whispers.

Unknown to the young man, the young lady had died suddenly earlier that night, and her father had gone to the next village to ask for help. The body had been arranged on her bed as if she was sleeping, and the door to the bedroom had been left unlocked. After several promptings and failed attempts at an embrace or a dialogue, the young man suspected his lover was playing pranks, angry at him for something he had said the last time they met. So in low tones and whispers, he started to apologize. Just then, it happened the young lady's father was returning from the other village. As he got closer, he heard voices coming from his dead daughter's bedroom. "That must be a ghost," he told himself. Feeling alone and afraid, the father made a noise by throwing an object against a wall inside the compound.

By that time, the young man, feeling the cold and stiff hands of his lover, had realized that all this while he had been trying to communicate with a dead person. He also became afraid, gripped with fear both from the fact he was sitting alone next to a dead body in a room and the thought he could be held responsible for his lover's death. He had to get away as quickly as possible. But the dead young lady's father was up and inside the compound of the house. The young man could also hear voices approaching the house. He felt trapped, cornered, and more afraid.

In a move marked with fear and desperation, the young man bolted out of the room toward the main entrance to the house. The dead woman's father, on seeing someone dashing from his dead daughter's bedroom, assumed it was her ghost and attempted to flee. The two men collided, got up without looking at or talking to each other, and headed in opposite directions of escape into the enveloping darkness.

The next morning, somebody discovered a drop of human excreta where the two men had collided the night before.

Question: who had left behind the little "piece of surprise"?

Chapter 14

Last Word—a Primer in Friendship and Good Neighborliness

The relationship among Akan Anyii-Baulé states can be summed up in one short phrase: peaceful coexistence and good neighborliness. Since their migration from what is today south-central Ghana beginning about the middle of the seventeenth century and over a period spanning a couple centuries, no Akan Anyii-Baulé group or tribe has acted aggressively toward another, whether in land and boundary disputes or other matters of competing national interests. Instead, dialogue, cooperation, and mutual respect are values that have guided every aspect of intertribal relations, including the resolution of seemingly difficult and intractable matters over which others have engaged in skirmishes or even gone to war. Nor has any Akan Anyii-Baulé tribe harbored any designs over territory or attempted to dominate another. The friendship, cooperation, and peaceful coexistence among the tribes is commendable considering that there are, at a minimum, forty identifiable subgroups that make up Akan Anyii-Baulé.

The bond among the tribes does not end at the superstructure or global level. Indeed, it plays out more at the micro and individual levels. Among Anyii-Baulé, there is a shared tradition called *Naa*. The best way to describe Naa is to say that it is intertribal jesting, a playful pulling of the leg of a member of one tribe by a member of another. The parties know the jokes are all for laughs, and none feels emotionally hurt by them. Naa is never intra-tribal, of two individuals of the same tribe making fun of each other. They are no doubt the only examples of Naa, but growing up, I heard the following often said to our Sahié (Sefwi) and Baulé (they call themselves Wawulé) neighbors, with the assumed inference our fellow Anyii-Baulé cousins are everything but smart.

The Man from Sahié (Sefwi) and His Shea Butter

There was this Sahié (Sefwi) trader who was going to market in the nearest big town on a very busy market day. He was carrying processed shea butter in an open container, which meant that his article of sale was exposed to the elements. Halfway to his destination, the skies opened up, soaking up the carrier and his luggage. Because he wanted to reach the market quickly in order to make good sales, Mr. Sahiéman refused to wait for the heavy downpour to subside or taper off. So on he went, and he finally got into town early enough. By this time, the rains had stopped, giving way to a hot tropical sunshine in the midafternoon when he arrived at market.

"But wait a minute," he told himself. "I cannot sell my shea butter all wet. I must have them dry the way I picked them up this morning." So in order to get his shea butter ready for buyers the way he wanted it, Mr. Sahiéman spread out the oil-based, soluble shea butter in the hot tropical sun, with the intention to dry off the rainwater. And there was a new word: melt! So the "wise" Mr. Sahiéman headed back home, bearing an empty container with residues of where balls of processed shea butter had been. He returned home with empty pockets, too.

The Hungry Baulé and the Bunches of Bananas

There was this Baulé man returning from the farm carrying a few bunches of ripe bananas. It was a long walk from the farm to town, and Mr. Baulé was tired not only from walking the distance but more from the heavy load of ripe bananas. He was hungry too and kept griping and complaining about being hungry. The interesting part is that Mr. Baulé owned the bananas he was carrying on an empty stomach for others to eat, even as he sweated and complained about being hungry! It never occurred to him he could solve his hunger pangs with a few of the bananas as well as lighten his burden. How bad could it get?

One Jab at the Anyii

The other tribes have jokes about the Anyii, but it seems the Anyii believe they are the smartest among Akan Anyii-Baulé who qualify to dish out the best Naa jokes all the time. But I remember being called an *ɛnyee* a few times, instead of Anyii, whenever I got on the nerves of a few Baulé friends. ɛnyee means python in almost all Akan Anyii-Baulé languages. Whatever the occasion, it is all banter and high fives anytime members of this branch of the Akan family get together. They look out for each other, too.

A further manifestation of the deep bond between members of Akan Anyii-Baulé tribes is that a quarrel or fight between individuals from opposite communities is considered a nonissue and treated with disdain. For example, if an Anyii and a Sefwi, Nzema or Baulé get into an argument or a fight, the elders will tell them to go make up and not waste anybody's time, and the two will have no choice but to apologize to each other and reconcile. It is unacceptable, or must I say a useless enterprise or even a sacrilege, to have two Anyii-Baulé tribes, communities, or individuals fighting each other to the point of becoming permanent adversaries or enemies. In the strict traditional sense, members from opposite sides of the group do not litigate, because they would be wasting each other's valuable time.

Akan Anyii-Baulé intertribal cooperation and peaceful coexistence can be attributed to the respective histories of the tribes when each group migrated from their ancestral home to avoid further family feuds. It seems each group swore never to relive the bitter historical experience where sibling fought sibling or, worse, became enemies. Because of the absence of tribal wars or aggression between them, Akan Anyii-Baulé structure of governance, unlike that of Akan Twi-Fante, is not based on military hierarchy. Where military action had become necessary in the past, as in for example Anyii Dwabene warriors going to war to rescue Abron Bonduku from Bouna aggression, or the same group raising a fighting force in the liberation effort in the War of Asikaso in 1898, popular mobilization has been the norm as opposed to falling on a regular, standing national army.

APPENDIX

Aspects of the Spoken Word

Earlier in this book, I mentioned that the Akan have been classified as belonging to two main language groups, namely Akan Twi-Fante and Akan Anyii-Baulé. I also mentioned that tribes and dialects constituting Akan Twi-Fante are almost all located in Ghana while about 70 percent of Akan Anyii-Baulé tribes and dialects are found in neighboring Cote d'Ivoire. Further, I linked the respective histories of Akan Anyii-Baulé to south-central Ghana where all, without exception, once called home.

As with every evolutionary process, time and space often shape and influence classes, groups, and species. In the cultural context particular to this book, I have identified the evolutionary process as the spoken word. Specifically, linguistic differentiation between the two Akan groups has been as a result of environmental dynamics as people migrated from the source to new locations. And the farther away people moved from the source or center, the greater the influence of new linguistic and cultural expression they have borrowed from new neighbors and others they met along the way. In other words, culture adapts in direct proportion to the pressure, dominant influence, and the willingness to embrace new thoughts and practices in a given geographical and political environment.

It is also true that cultural evolution occurs even in sedentary societies insofar as those societies interact with others from outside their immediate communities or adapt to environmental changes. The environmental changes may be voluntary, invasive, or coercive. It may be a mutually shared experience or one where a dominant culture influences or assimilates a weaker one. A dominant culture may influence or assimilate a weaker one by way of the arts, trade, commerce, scholarship, scientific advancement, or by conquest through sheer force of arms. In the last example, however, a conquered people would always want to set themselves free, now or in the future. One constant is that time has been the main driver of change, and time is not at rest. Therefore, all elements dependent on time are fluid, in constant change, motion, self-adjustment, and adaptation.

I submit that at some point in their respective histories, either as belonging to one monolithic group or as close neighbors, one to the other, most Akan Twi-Fante and Anyii-Baulé tribes spoke the same language. But as people moved away to form new groups and those that remained regrouped, each group redefined itself and was affected and sometimes influenced by new neighbors in the environment. It is also true that the farther away groups moved from the source, origin, or center, the wider the gap and greater the alienation in the spoken word and cultural expression, generally.

When the Baulé coined their name from Baa Wule, meaning "The Child Died," they were speaking the same language as the kinsfolk they had left not so long ago at Nsuta in Asante. The history of the Baulé is that they were on the run from Nsuta when at a point, their leader, Abena Pokua, had to sacrifice her little child to the river god in order for her people to get to the opposite bank. The root statement that defined Baulé identity is reasonable evidence the Asante of the eighteenth century spoke a language or dialect similar to Baulé and by extension, Anyii. It is further evidence the language that became known as Asante Twi evolved several decades after the respective departures of the Baulé and Anyii from what is now south-central Ghana. In fact, older generation Asante admit the tribe "used to speak differently several generations ago."

It is generally accepted that among Anyii-Baulé languages, Wassa, Sefwi, and Anyii remain closest to Twi. The reason may be attributed to the fact that each of the three Anyii-Baulé tribes either shares traditional borders with one or more Akan Twi-Fante tribes and is therefore within close range of influence, or that members of the tribe migrated most recently. Though Nzema and Ahanta share borders with Fante (and in the peculiar case of Ahanta, they have in fact, been eaten up by the Fante immigrants), these last two surprisingly are farther away from Twi than their first three tribal cousins.

In the following list of examples, I have chosen words and expressions common to Wassa, Sefwi, and Anyii to illustrate the linguistic connection and similarity between Akan Anyii-Baulé and Akan Twi-Fante. In so doing, I have sought a standard form of usage common to or understood by a majority of Anyii-Baulé speakers.

A key linguistic difference between Akan Twi-Fante and Akan Anyii-Baulé is that Twi and Fante (Fantse, Mfantse) consonants are hard in relation to Anyii-Baulé. For example, names and words beginning with the letters *k, s, t,* and *f* in Twi are usually *g, z, d,* and *v,* respectively, in Anyii-Baulé. I illustrate with a few examples:

Anyii-Baulé	Twi-Fante	English
Ahenvié	Ahenfié	palace (of a chief/king)
Amamvo	Amamfo	a name
Amanvoso	Amamfoso	fort (as in old, abandoned settlement or town)
Angama	Ankama/Ankoma	a name
Nguluma	Nkruma	okro/okra
Ngalaa	Nkra	farewell, message
Ngwandaa	Nkwanta	junction, crossroad
Ngala Ngwandaa	Nkra Nkwanta	name of a town
Ngateɛ	Nkateɛ	groundnuts/peanuts
Nyandakyi	Nyantakyi	a name
Nza	Nsa	the number three
Nzaa	Nsaa	traditional funeral donation
Nzia	Nsia	six (as in number); also, a name
Nzué (Nzema: Nzulɛ)	Nsuo	Water

While Akan Anyii-Baulé employs what I will call "joined and heavy" consonants, these do not exist in Akan Twi-Fante. Specifically, *kp* and *gb* conjoined as a word or part of a word is alien to Akan Twi-Fante word structure and formation. For example:

Anyii-Baulé	Twi-Fante	English
Wɔ nwo te sɛɛ? Me nwo te **kp**aa	Wo ho te sɛn? Me ho yɛ paa	How are you? I am doing fine. Where "kpaa" in Anyii-Baulé means fine, good or okay.
A**kp**oɛ	Obotan	rock
"**Kp**agya." Also "ma so"	"Pagya"; also "ma so"	lift (an object)
Kpɔmaa	Poma	staff (as in walking stick)
M**gb**ɔma	Ampoma	A name. Ampoma is one of the unisex names among the Twi. For Anyii-Baulé, Mgbɔma is a female name.

It is sometimes difficult to tell by looks or body language between members from the two groups, but an Anyii-Baulé can easily tell an Akan Twi-Fante, when the former hears someone saying, "me nwo te *kwaa*," instead of "me nwo te *kpaa*," meaning, "I am doing fine." Just as when a typical Frenchman would say, "I'm appy," where he would like to say, "I'm happy," because the letter *h* is silent in French.

Most nouns in Anyii-Baulé have the suffix "lɛ." For example: *kalɛ* (*ɛka* or *ka*; debt); *yalɛ* (*yeaw* or *yaw*; sorrow); *anwonyalɛ* (*yadeɛ*; sickness or infirmity). In the same format, we have *awiélеɛ* (*awiéɛ*; the end, or destiny).

Anyii-Baulé seldom use the letter *r*. Where it is *r* in Akan Twi-Fante, it is more likely than not *l* in Akan Anyii-Baulé. For example:

Anyii-Baulé	Twi-Fante	English
Abɛlɛbɛ	Aborɔbɛ	pineapple
Kulo	Kuro	town/city
Ngalaa	Nkra	farewell, message
Palako	Prako	pig/hog
Bala	Bra	come

While some words, object names, and expressions have changed or taken on slightly different meanings in the two classified Akan groups over the years, a great deal remain the same or similar, a constant reminder of a historical relationship. In many cases, words or names of objects considered classical in Twi are in contemporary use among Anyii-Baulé tongues, and vice versa.

With Akan Twi-Fante as the older and therefore more complex in terms of diction, political organization, and cultural expression, it is not surprising or uncommon for the speaker among Akan Anyii-Baulé to regularly defer to the Twi roots of the meanings of words and as point of reference. For example, I have demonstrated elsewhere in this book that though Anyii-Baulé day names are different from those of Akan Twi-Fante and hardly reflect associated kra da or what are sometimes referred to as common names, parents in the former group name their infants in accordance with Twi-Fante usage. For ease of reference, I reproduce below the list of day names:

	Day Name (Anyii)	Day Name (Twi)	Female Child (Anyii)	Female Child (Twi)	Male Child (Anyii)	Male Child (Twi)
Monday	Kisié	Dwoada	Adwa	Adwoa	Kwadwo	Kwadwo
Tuesday	Dwɛlɛ	Benada	Abana (nasal)	Abena	Kwabana	Kwabena
Wednesday	Manlaa	Wukuada	Akua/Ahu	Akua	Kwaku	Kwaku
Thursday	Wuhue	Yawoada	Yaa/Aya	Yaa	Kwaw/Yaw	Yaw
Friday	Yaa	Fiada	Afua/Afue	Afua/Afia	Kofi	Kofi
Saturday	Fue	Memeneda	Ama/Amoa (nasal)	Ama	Kwame	Kwame
Sunday	Molɛ	Kwasiada	Akwasi/ Akisi/ Akosua	Akosua	Kwasi	Kwasi

A comparative list of a few flora and fauna:

Anyii-Baulé	Twi-Fante	English
Abɔɔngaa	Aborankaa or Ankaa	orange
Adoa	Adowa	duiker
Dwéé	Adwene	fish
Akaatia	Akaatia	chimpanzee
Akoo	Ako	parrot
Akyekyele	Akyekyedeɛ	tortoise
Anomaa	Anoma	bird
Apatupélé	Apatuprɛ́	a type of bird
Atadwe	Atadwe	tiger nut
Awéé/Ayéé	Abɛ	palm
Bénzé	Bénsé	iguana
Boté/Kusié	Kusié	giant rat
Bowué	Béwuo	thorn or bone
Ehoɛ	Ekɔɔ	buffalo
Elɛngyɛ	Dɛnkyɛm	crocodile
Enyaa	Onyina	silk cotton tree
Epɛtɛ	Pɛtɛ/ɔpɛtɛ	vulture

Esoe	Osono	elephant
Ewoo	ɔwɔ	snake
Gyara	Gyata	lion
Kétéboɛ	Kétébɔ/ɔtwee	antelope
Kɔkɔte	Kɔkɔte	swine, wild hog/pig
Kubé/Agyéé	Kubé	coconut (tree or the fruit)
Kukuba/Kpulé	Kukuban/Opuro	squirrel
Kutukwaku	Kutukwaku	hyena
Kwabalafo	Kwabrafo	grizzly bear
Kwakué	Kwakuo	green monkey
Kwaakwaadabi	Kwaakwaadabi	crow
Mangani	Mankani	cocoyam
Mmae	Mmane	herrings
Niné	Miré	mushroom
Nyamaa	Ahoma	climber; also, rope
Pɛnzɛɛ	Apɛsɛ	porcupine
Tweapea	Tweapea	a type of chewing stick

A few general names and words in comparison:

Anyii-Baulé	Twi-Fante	English
Nyamea	Nyame	God (Creator God)
Dangama	Ɔdomankoma	Omnipotent Creator
Nyilaa	Nhyira	blessing
Nyilaa	Awadegyaeɛ	divorce
Elui	Dui or Odum	name of a tree
Elubo (Elui-Bo)	Odumase (Odum-Ase)	name of a town
Kumbo (Kum-Bo)	Kumase (Kum-ase)	Though Kumase in Asante translates into Anyii-Baulé as Kum-Bo, the Akan Twi-Fante reference has been retained.
Kɔmea	Kɔmfoɔ	fetish priest
Yɔboɛ	ɔboɔ	stone
Ngyɛsea	Nwansena	housefly
Abusua	Abusua	extended family
Sikaa	Sika	money (also, name for gold)
Asukotwa	Asukotwa	snow
Asorɔkye	Asorɔkye	waves (as in sea waves)
Nangoloma	Kotodwe (Fante: Nankroma)	knee
Yakɔ	Yaakɔ	my condolences

Ehiaa	Ohia	poverty
Akwaaba	Akwaaba	welcome
Amaneɛ	Amaneɛ	Literally, "reason of visit." Traditional protocol among all Akan groups requires visitors or returnees from a journey to inform purpose of visit or give account of trip they're returning from.
Ewia	Awia	sun
Nzalamaa	Nsoroma	stars
Sala/Sra	ɔsranee/ɔsram/Bosome	moon/month
Bɔfoɛ/Bɔmɔfoɛ	Bɔfoɔ/Bɔmɔfoɔ	hunter
Bɔfoɛ	Bɔfoɔ	Creator (as in Creator God)
Bayé	Bayié	witchcraft
Atee (sounds like "ateen")	ɔkwan	path, way, road
Kyéré me atee	Kyerematen means Kyere me kwan	Show me the way / Lead me. A popular Twi name.
Aseɛ	Asase	earth, land
Ennɛ	Ennɛ	today
Anoma	Enora	yesterday
Ehema	ɔkyena	tomorrow

Afoɛ	Afe	year
Nyanzoa	Nyanso/Aniwuo	shame
Kalataa/Fuluwa	Krataa	book. "Kalataa/Krataa" is borrowed from the Spanish "Carta."
Mgba	Mpa	bed
Bomo/Kundu	Bomo/Kuntu	blanket
Mgbaboa/Mmaboa	Mpaboa	footwear
Sékaa	Afe	comb
Tui	Tuo/Etuo	gun
Bia	Akonwa/Akongwa	chair
Kanea	Kanea	lantern/lamp
Sumi	Sumiɛ	pillow
Dadeɛ/Kué	Sekan/Nkrantɛ/Dadeɛ	cutlass
Ateɛ	Atere	spoon
Nwomaa	Nwoma/Nhoma	book/hide (as in animal hide)
Akonda	Akonta	brother-in-law
Me sia	M'ase	my mother/father-in-law
Biésua/Nyii/Nyima	Barima/Nini	Male
Balaa	Baa/ɔbaa/Bedeɛ	Female
Sanvɛ	Safoa	Key

Some common statements and proverbs:

Anyii-Baulé	Twi-Fante	English
M'anu me nwo	M'anu me ho	I have regretted.
Ye nwunu agu ase	N'anim agu ase/N'ani awu	S/he is ashamed.
Anoma Sandrofia. ɛfa ye a, afa musué. Ɛyakyi ye a, ayakyi saleɛ	Anoma Santrofié. Wofa no a, wo afa musuo. Wo gya no a, wo agyae sradeɛ	Sandrofia (Anyii) or Santrofié (Twi), the proverbial bird that is a curse if taken home, and a loss of good nutrition if left in the bush. In other words, a catch-22 situation.
Wa fa ye ti nu	Afa ne tiri mu	S/he is disoriented.
Bié afa ye nye so	Ebi afa n'ani so	S/he has learned her/his lesson.
Wɔ nwo te sɛɛ?	Wo ho te sɛn?	How are you?
Wɔ ni wɔ bɛlɛ?	Wo ni wɔ hɔ?	Is your mother home?
Wɔ se wɔ bɛlɛ?	Wo se wɔ hɔ?	Is your father home?
Na me ɔ	ɛnyɛ me a	It is not my fault; I didn't do it.
Na wɔ ɔ	ɛnyɛ wo a	It's not your fault/I don't blame you; You didn't do it.
Me te bɔ ɛka ne	Me te nea wo re ka no	I understand what you're saying.
Me sɛ/so ba	Me re ba	I'm on my way.
Me sɛ/so kɔ	Me re kɔ	I'm leaving. I'm on my way out.

Wa nwuna nwuna me	Wa huna huna me	She/He/It has scared me.
Me da wɔ ase	Me da wo ase	I thank you.
Me yɛ wɔ mo	Me ma wo amo	I greet you. I thank you.
Mua wɔ noa	Mua w'ano	Keep quiet; don't say anything; shut up.
Na su	Ensu	Don't cry.
Yakyi/yaki sulɛ	Gyae suu	Stop crying.
Yakyi/yaki me	Gyae me	Leave me; leave me alone.
Ma me bié	Ma me bi	Give me some; share with me.
Su bié ma me	Su bi ma me	Cry with me; show empathy to me.
Me nye aboro	M'ani abere	I'm serious; I'm in mourning.
Me sɛlɛ na m'adi	Me srɛ na m'adi	I'm desperate; I'm down on my knees.
Wa hia me	Ahia me	I've nothing; I'm poor.
Nzu?	ɛdeɛn/adɛn?	What/why?
Nzu yeɛ wayɔ wɔ ɔ?	ɛdeɛn na ayɛ wo?	What has happened to you?
Nzu ahe? Nzu koso ahe?	ɛdeɛn ni? ɛdeɛn nso ni?	What is this? What is all this?
Nzu ti yeɛ me nyɔ ye pɛɛko ɔ?	Adɛn nti na me nyɛ no prɛko/Adɛn na me nyɛ no prɛko?	Why can't I do it now?
Nwa?	Hwan?	Who?

Nwa deε ɔ?	Hwan de a?	Whose is it?
Ye lε nwa?	ɔne hwan?	Who is s/he? (confrontational)
Nwa ɔ?	Hwan a?	Who is s/he? (nonconfrontational)
εtole nwa?	Wo too hwan?	Who did you meet?
εkyéré wɔ nwo	Wo kyerε wo ho/Wo dua wɔ ho bɔɔ	You are arrogant; you are full of yourself.
εkyéré wɔ now somaa	Wo kyerε wo ho dodo/Wo dua wo ho bɔɔ dodo	You are too arrogant; you are too difficult.
Wɔ wɔ ni?	ɔwɔ he?	Where is s/he?
εwɔ ni?	wo wɔ he?	Where are you?
Ma soma ye	Ma soma no	I've sent him/her on an errand.
Ni lε wa?	εhe ne ha?	I dare you!
Me ngome	Me nkoaa	Just me; I'm alone.
Wa ha me ngome	Aka me nko	I'm only one left.
Me wu a, na su	Me wu a, nsu	Literally, "Don't weep the day I die." But it's an expression meaning "I'm eternally grateful."
Me te wɔ ni/Wɔ ni lε me	Me yε wo ni/Wo ni ne me	I am your mother.
Me te wɔ se/Wɔ se lε me	Me yε wo se/Wo se ne me	I am your father.
Me kpɔma wɔ atwɛleε	Mε poma wo twεdeε	I'll punch your head.

Me da wɔ noa ase	Me da w'ano ase	Thank you for the kind words.
ɛne Nyamea hɔ	ɛne Nyame/Onyame nkɔ	Godspeed; may God be with you.
Nyamea gyina wɔ si	Nyame/Onyame nyina w'akyi	May God be your supporter.
Nyamea te me bɔfoɛ	Nyame/Onyame ne me bɔfo	God is my creator.

The Ubiquitous "Bɛ" Third-Person Plural Pronoun

I would like to briefly explore a few other aspects of language structure between the two Akan family groups, namely Akan Twi-Fante and Akan Anyii-Baulé. An understanding of the language structure of each group is important to a better appreciation of usage, similarity, and convergence. As a key foundation of culture and the medium by which a group defines and projects a collective worldview and how it relates to the rest of the world, the spoken word interprets and actualizes a people. Civilization cannot exist without culture; in fact, civilization is culture. As the root or foundation of culture, the level of sophistication of a particular language is indicative of the civilization it supports. In other words, the level of a given civilization is in direct relationship to the evolution of the spoken word that supports it.

All Akan Anyii-Baulé tribes, without exception, employ the third-person plural pronoun *bɛ*. Bɛ equates the English "they" (subjective pronoun), "them" (objective pronoun), and "their" or "theirs" (possessive pronoun). The corresponding pronoun for much of Akan Twi-Fante tribes is *wɔn, wɔɔmo*, or *hɔn*.

Among Akan Twi-Fante tribes, the various Bono subgroups use the bɛ plural pronoun just as among Anyii-Baulé tribes. Other Akan Twi-Fante who, it seems, have limited knowledge and appreciation of the evolution of the various Akan language groups, both Twi-Fante and Anyii-Baulé, tend to amuse themselves with the unique Bono application of the bɛ pronoun as part of Akan Twi-Fante language structure. But these could be on the wrong side of history, language evolution, and cultural dynamics. Let us examine some common historical facts about the Akan that may throw some light on the subject of linguistic evolution.

It is quite plausible that all, or at least much of, Akan Twi-Fante used bɛ as a plural pronoun in time past. It is easy to understand why. Much of the collective Akan civilization originated from Begho, a town located immediately south of the Black Volta. Later, Bonomanso, also located south of the Black Volta but closer to present-day Takyiman, succeeded Begho in the formation of collective Akan culture and civilization. Begho was one of the major kingdoms in the West African subregion that succeeded ancient Ghana Empire further west. As were Begho and Bonomanso, Takyiman is also located in the administrative region called Brong Ahafo, in present-day Ghana.

As early as the twelfth century AD, Begho was already a thriving commercial center that brought together traders from the Sahara and their counterparts from the forest region to the south. Gold, ivory, leather, salt, cola nuts, cloth, and copper alloys were the main articles of trade. It is also true that most if not all Akan groups migrated from Begho and Bonomanso. In recognition of the historical fact that Bono was home to, and before all others, Akan everywhere refer to a "Bono Abakan," which means "Bono, the first born," or "Bono, our elder sibling."

Among Akan Twi-Fante languages, Bono is unique in the use of the plural pronoun bɛ. Since Bono is recognized and acknowledged as the oldest Akan subgroup, it is reasonable to say that the Bono version of Akan Twi-Fante was original language, from which others evolved into new forms, and not vice versa. It is also reasonable to say that since all Akan Anyii-Baulé not only migrated from what is now south-central Ghana but also employ the bɛ pronoun in their respective languages, the language in use at the time of their respective migrations had bɛ to denote "they" and "them." From above analysis, it is further reasonable to suggest that the shift from bɛ to wɔn, wɔɔmo, or hɔn among other Akan Twi-Fante languages was a later linguistic dynamic in the evolution and usage among the various Akan Twi-Fante groups.

It is therefore safe to conclude that the plural pronoun bɛ is as old and authentic as the foundations of the Akan people and their civilization, dating back to ancient Begho and Bonomanso. It is also safe to conclude that the Bono, through linguistic expression and geographical location, are a significant link between modern and ancient Akan cultures and a strong and trusted bridge between Akan Anyii-Baulé and Akan Twi-Fante.

ACKNOWLEDGMENTS

They are no longer with us and therefore not aware, in the physical sense, of this book, but in their memory is due a deserving recognition and gratitude. Though they had been treated unfairly and unjustly, they chose migration where others would have taken up arms. I salute Anyii Dwabene Kwasi and his pioneer supporters for their politics of nonviolence about three and a half centuries ago. They restrained themselves in a time and epoch when might was right. Perhaps it is this level of maturity and sophistication, which abhors violence, that informed their choice of name as Anyii, which is derived from the statement: "Bɛ wo yɛ, hene y'Anyi" ("We were mature or precocious, even at birth"). Truly wise, they were. I would be telling a different story today, if at all, had Nana Kwasi and his council of pace-setter elders failed to properly manage anger in the face of injustice and provocation.

Next, I would like to recognize Nana Bredu Asamandje and his liberating warriors on the plains of Abron Bonduku. Nanammɔ, you saved a nation when you did not have to. But for your love of freedom and liberty, and your abhorrence of the unjust and bully, you saved Abron and restored her wounded pride and dignity. You were brave men of a powerful nation who preferred to use strength to defend and protect the weak against aggressors and opportunism. You demonstrated to neighbors and the world at large that peace, and the pursuit and enforcement of it, is a necessary value that must endure and supersede all others. Anyii Dwabene history could not have been prouder without you.

Nkrankwanta is Anyii Dwabene Kotoko, and Anyii Dwabene Kotoko is of the larger Akan Oyoko abusua family whose totem is the falcon. To you, beloved Junction Town, a big hug of *mmo*, or well done for establishing a new community of hope and possibilities to all. Brave men and women who left everything behind for the sake of liberty and dignity, I thank you for teaching that it is more honorable to choose freedom with little over servitude in relative abundance.

I am able to tell the story of Nkrankwanta and Anyii Dwabene because a few individuals dedicated part of their lives to not only preserve in memory the people's story but also made conscious efforts to pass on the knowledge to generations down the line. Among these individuals, I would be remiss if I did not mention Granduncle Ali Kwadwo Nziah, fetish priest, herbalist, historian, chief linguist, and muezzin. Grandma Afua Seala (a.k.a. Hajia Masara) of blessed memory, I thank you for ensuring that I received the best in formal education as well as sharing the Anyii Kotoko family history. You both have helped in no small way to keeping alive the fascinating stories that inspired the publication of *Cultural Migration: A short History of Nkrankwanta and Anyii Dwabene.*

My mother, Akwasi Somala (a.k.a. Hajia Amina), has provided detailed info on the two ruling houses of Nkrankwanta, namely Nziah Akpau and Ngessah Aku. An accomplished Abodaa dancer in her younger days, she reviewed my draft presentation on Anyii traditional dances and songs. I am thankful, *Mmo* (Mother).

Kwame Anane Adjei is a royal of Dormaa and a good friend. When I needed more information regarding the piece on the history of Dormaaman, Kwame was ever ready to consult for free. All I needed to do was to make a trip to his Toronto home, which he shares with wife, Julie, and son, Junior. I am grateful to the Anane Adjei family of Toronto, Canada.

Cultural Migration: A short History of Nkrankwanta and Anyii Dwabene chronicles, among other topics, the success story of Nkrankwanta. As a town and community, the founder Anyii Dwabene could not have done it all alone without the active participation and contributions of newer and arriving townfolks. Therefore, Cocoa Town is what she is because of the collective effort of all who have made it their permanent home and contributed in many ways toward her rapid growth and development. The immigrant town that it is, Nkrankwanta continues to attract and welcome all. I thank all for being good and faithful to Nkrankwanta.

While I share with others the success or credit for *Cultural Migration: A Short History of Nkrankwanta and Anyii Dwabene*, I take full responsibility for any errors, omissions, or other shortcomings that this book may contain. It is only reasonable to say that I cannot fault others for any misrepresentation in my telling the story of my people.

Ultimately, all glory and praises are to God Almighty.

NOTES AND REFERENCES

Preface

p. 6   Regarding the history of Anyii Dwabene Sié,
Koffi (1976). Les Agni-Diabè, Histoire et Societé.
Université de Paris I Pantheon–Sorbonne.

Chapter 1—The Name of a People

p. 10   Akan languages under two main groups,
namely Twi-Fante, and Anyii-Baulé.
Abakah, Emmanuel Nicholas. *Hypotheses on the
Diachronic Development of the Akan Language
Group*, p. 10. University of Education, Winneba,
http://llacan.vjf.cnrs.fr/fichiers/nigercongo/
fichiers/abakah_akan.pdf.

p. 11   Recent census figures put Akans at a little
over 47 (47.3) percent of total population of
Ghana.
Ghana Statistical Service (May 2013). *2010
Population & Housing Census: National Analytical
Report*, p. 61,
http://www.statsghana.gov.gh/docfiles/2010phc/
National_Analytical_Report.pdf.

p. 11   In Cote d'Ivoire, Akan constitute about 42 percent of total population.
Wikipedia, https://en.wikipedia.org/wiki/C%C3% B4te_d%27Ivoire#Demographics.

p. 11   Chokosi is a small Akan group in northern Togo whose members are believed to have migrated from Anyii Annɔ in Cote d'Ivoire; they refer to themselves as Annɔfoɛ (Twi: Annɔfoɔ), or "People of Annɔ."
Wikipedia, https://en.wikipedia.org/wiki/ Chakosi_people
Twi.bb (online dictionary for the Twi language of the Akan people of Ghana in West Africa): *Chokosi.*   http://www.twi.bb/akan-people-chokosi.php.

Chapter 2—Migration from Amansie
p. 15   Several Francophone researchers and oral historians in Cote d'Ivoire have referred to a place called Assuamara or Assuémara, north of Dankira
Sié, Koffi (1976). *Les Agni-Diabè, Histoire et Societé*, pp. 35, 36. Université de Paris I Pantheon–Sorbonne.

p. 16   It is more likely Kwasi and his followers left Dwaben in Amansie earlier than 1697. The migration could have happened in or about 1670, at the beginning of the reign of Nana Adarkwa Yiadom, the first Dwabenhene (king of a united Dwaben state), who ruled from 1670 to 1715.

Ghana Traditional Polities, http://www. worldstatesmen.org/Ghana_native.html.

p. 16   Interestingly, a group in Ghana that calls itself Asante Dwaben (and by extension New Dwaben, a breakaway group from Asante Dwaben) traces its origins to the Amansie area about the same time as Kwasi and his people were there.
Manhyia Archives, http://manhyiaarchives.com/page.php?id=5.

p. 17   A blogger who goes by the name Akrase, a son of Asante Dwaben, writes as follows:
"In fact, Dwabens aren't situate (sic) in Ghana only. In La Cote d'Ivoire, they can be found in large nos., in Assikasou."
Note: First royal capital of Anyii Dwabene was Asikaso (founded by Brédou Asamandje in 1750), until King Anyini Bilé the First moved to a new capital of AnyiniBilékro, in 1880. Asikaso still exists but as a small town within a few miles from AnyiniBilékro.
Akrase. *A focus on Juaben (Dwaben) its chiefs and queens,*
http://akrase.blogspot.ca/2007/07/focus-on-juaben-dwaben-its-chiefs-and.html.

p. 17   But in 1832, Asante attacked Dwaben over suspicions the latter had collaborated with the enemy when in the battle of Akatamanso.
Addo-Fening, R. (June 1973). *Asante Refugees in Akyem Abuakwa 1875–1912*, pp. 39–64,

Transactions of the Historical Society of Ghana, vol. 14, no. 1.

p. 17   Nana Kwaku Boateng, the Dwaben king, and several followers, took refuge in Akyem Abuakwa in south-central Ghana. In 1841, reconciliation was struck at a meeting at Kumase between Asante (the confederacy) and Dwaben (an autonomous member of confederacy). However, between 1875 and 1876, and for the second time, the Dwaben returned as refugees to Akyem Abuakwa.
Addo-Fening, R. (June 1973). *Asante Refugees in Akyem Abuakwa 1875–1912*, pp. 39–64, Transactions of the Historical Society of Ghana, vol. 14, no. 1.

p. 18   ... they were joined by other Asante refugees from Afigyaase and Asokore.
Addo-Fening, R. (June 1973). *Asante Refugees in Akyem Abuakwa 1875–1912*, pp. 39–64, Transactions of the Historical Society of Ghana, vol. 14, no. 1.

p. 20   "The three states of Sefwi share a common culture in spite of the fact that they all came from different places ... In the worship of the tutelar deity Soborε, the three states also have a common identity. The deity is supposed not only to protect the states from all calamities but it is also a fertility god."

Daaku, K.Y., *A History of Sefwi: A Survey of Oral Evidence*, p. 32, Michigan State University Libraries, http://archive.lib.msu.edu/DMC/African%20 Journals/pdfs/Institue%20of%20African%20 Studies%20Research%20Review/1971v7n3/ asrv007003003.pdf.

Chapter 3—War between Bouna and Abron Bonduku
p. 21   The Abron king at the time is believed to have been Nana Kofi Sono, who ruled from 1746 to 1760.
Ghana   Traditional   Polities,   http://www. worldstatesmen.org/Ghana_native.html.

Chapter 4—A New Nation Is Born
p. 26   But in 1880, Anyini Bilé I (the seventh occupant of the Anyii Dwabene stool), moved the capital from Asikaso to his rubber plantation at Anyini-Bilé-Kro (Anyini Bilé Town).
Sié, Koffi (1976). *Les Agni-Diabè, Histoire et Societé*, pp. 56–60, 68. Université de Paris I Pantheon–Sorbonne.

p. 26   ... list of Anyii Dwabene Brembi (Twi: Amanhene), or kings.
Sié, Koffi (1976). *Les Agni-Diabè, Histoire et Societé*, p. 56. Université de Paris I Pantheon–Sorbonne.

Chapter 5—War of Asikaso: April 29–July 2, 1898

p. 32   Yaw Fum was at once young, rich, outgoing, eloquent, cosmopolitan, brave, and had grown extremely popular with the "pɔyɛfoɛ" (rubber latex collectors) and the youth, in general.

Sié, Koffi (1976). *Les Agni-Diabè, Histoire et Societé*, pp. 60, 61. Université de Paris I Pantheon–Sorbonne.

p. 33   The new king ruled from Tengualan, a town he had earlier founded and where he was chief prior to ascending the higher Anyii Dwabene stool.

Sié, Koffi (1976). *Les Agni-Diabè, Histoire et Societé*, pp. 60, 61. Université de Paris I Pantheon–Sorbonne.

p. 33   Among Brembi (King) Yaw Fum's collaborators were a few Dwabene chiefs, notable among them Nanou (chief of Manzanouan), Anyimu (chief of Anwaafutu), Boadu (chief of Nyandaa), and Aforo (chief of Dame).

Sié, Koffi (1976). *Les Agni-Diabè, Histoire et Societé*, pp. 128, 129, 141, 146, 156, 159. Université de Paris I Pantheon–Sorbonne.

p. 33   … across the frontier in the Gold Coast, Yaw Fum had a strong ally in the person of Kwadwo Adabo, who is believed to have founded Adabokro (Adabo Town), a bustling Esahie (Sefwi) town on the northern reaches of what is now the Western Region of Ghana.

Sié, Koffi (1976). *Les Agni-Diabè, Histoire et Societé*, pp. 146, 149, 151, 156. Université de Paris I Pantheon–Sorbonne.

p. 32   … the colonial administration and the State of Dwabene had signed a treaty back in 1892 to, among other things, allow a French outpost at Asikaso.
Sié, Koffi (1976). *Les Agni-Diabè, Histoire et Societé*, p. 200. Université de Paris I Pantheon–Sorbonne.

p. 34   On June 18, 1897, a day to be remembered as a breaking point of the beginning of hostilities between Yaw Fum and the French colonialists, a delegation of administrators had travelled up from the colonial capital on the coast with new decrees they wanted Dwabene indigenes to obey. King Yaw Fum, feeling insulted and belittled, would not oblige and said so in no uncertain terms …
Sié, Koffi (1976). *Les Agni-Diabè, Histoire et Societé*, p. 135. Université de Paris I Pantheon–Sorbonne.

p. 35   Early in the morning of April 29, 1898, and without warning, armed young men in battle gear surrounded and laid Siége to the French outpost at Asikaso.
Sié, Koffi (1976). *Les Agni-Diabè, Histoire et Societé*, p. 138, 173. Université de Paris I Pantheon–Sorbonne.

p. 35   The strategy was effective initially, because it is reported that the besieged, at some point, resorted to cooking leaves for dinner and squeezing drinking water out of plantain stalks.
Sié, Koffi (1976). *Les Agni-Diabè, Histoire et Societé*, p. 153. Université de Paris I Pantheon–Sorbonne.

p. 36   … a breakthrough for the French side finally came when reinforcements arrived from Bingerville, in the form of the dreaded and battle-tested battalion of Senegalese sharpshooters popularly known as *tirailleurs sénégalais*. The ferocity of this colonial special forces who later distinguished themselves on the battlefields of Europe and Indochina made all the difference at Asikaso.
Sié, Koffi (1976). *Les Agni-Diabè, Histoire et Societé*, p. 157. Université de Paris I Pantheon–Sorbonne.

p. 36   … though they had stood tall and gallantly for what they believed was in defense of nation and dignity, the Dwabene combatants fell short in the long run, and on July 2, 1898, their resolve buckled, and they fell to superior French firepower and battlefield tactical discipline.
Sié, Koffi (1976). *Les Agni-Diabè, Histoire et Societé*, pp. 138, 173. Université de Paris I Pantheon–Sorbonne.

p. 36   … a hasty trial was organized by the victorious French army, and on July 9, 1898, Yaw Fum, king of Anyii Dwabene, along with Nanou (chief of Manzanouan) and Boadu (chief of Nyandaa) were condemned to death and executed by firing squad.

Sié, Koffi (1976). *Les Agni-Diabè, Histoire et Societé*, p. 164. Université de Paris I Pantheon–Sorbonne.

p. 37   The execution of the king and two of his prominent chiefs has, to this day, remained a state oath and a taboo to Anyii Dwabene, so that to invoke "Alaka Nza" (Twi: "Nnakaa Mɛɛnsa," The Three Coffins), in reference to the three coffins that bore the dead bodies of the executed king and two prominent chiefs of Anyii Dwabene …

Sié, Koffi (1976). *Les Agni-Diabè, Histoire et Societé*, p. 164. Université de Paris I Pantheon–Sorbonne.

Chapter 6—Migration from Kotokoso

p. 39   The structure of Native Administration, especially as practiced in British West Africa, was premised on working in partnership with a few powerful chiefs and kings or their chosen educated African representatives. The arrangement is sometimes referred to as "indirect rule."

Crowder, Michael (July 1964). *Indirect Rule: French and British Style*. Vol. 34, No. 3, pp.

197–205. *Africa: Journal of the International African Institute.* Cambridge University Press.

p. 40 "In 1900, the French sought to levy a head tax on the entire population and three years later began the construction of a railway which required the seizing of African lands, and increased demands for slave labour. The tax was a total reversal of Afro-French relations as governed by the treaties. Prior to 1900 the French were tribute-paying aliens; by the new tax law they became conquerors exacting a tribute from their former masters.

… In 1916 the Baulé led another uprising which came almost as close as that of 1908 to expelling the French. In 1917 in hopeless despair of victory the Agni (a people closely related to the Asante) migrated as a body to the less harsh colonialism of the British in neighbouring Ghana."

Webster, J.B. and Boahen, Adu (1967). *The Growth of African Civilization: The Revolutionary Years—West Africa Since 1800,* pp. 250, 251. Longmans.

p. 42 The Dormaa had earlier migrated to the Amansie area from Akwamu, in the neighborhood of River Volta, south of the Afram Plains.

Akwamuman: The History of Dormaa and the Akwamu Connection,

http://akwamuman.org/test/index.php?option=com_content&view=article&id=79:dormaa&catid=42:history&Itemid=29.

Chapter 8—Anyii Kotoko Stool

p. 53 The eight Akan Abusua, in random order, are …

Ossei-Akoto, Baafuor. *The 8 Akan Abusua*. http://asanteman.freeservers.com/custom.html

Twi.bb (online dictionary for the Twi language of the Akan people of Ghana in West Africa): *Abusua*. http://www.twi.bb/akan-abusua.php.

pp. 62 & 67 **enstool/ment:** The process of crowning a new king or chief among the Akan people. A specially carved and darkened stool is the primary source of traditional authority among the Akan.

destool/ment: The process of removing traditional authority and power from an individual who had earlier been crowned king or chief; dethroning an Akan king or chief.

p. 68 The Anyii Indenie, immediate southern neighbors to Anyii Dwabene, also migrated from Asante for the sake of peace.

Histoire du royaume de l'Indénié, http://bellecotedivoire.com/abengourou.php?id=161&titre_article=histoire-du-royaume-de-l-indenie.

p. 68 Notable examples are the Baulé of Cote d'Ivoire who in the eighteenth century and under the leadership of their matriarch and later queen, Abena Pokua, left Nsuta and Mampong areas of Asante to avoid in-fighting among branches of the same extended family.

The narration continues that soon after Abena Pokua had thrown her child into the fast-flowing big river, an army of crocodiles lined up, jaw to tail, across the width of the river, forming a dangling reptilian bridge, upon which the Nsuta emigrants gingerly walked to safety. Henceforward, the group called itself "Baa Wule," meaning, "The Child Died," hence Baulé. In other words, Abena Pokua sacrificed her only child for the sake of her people and the new Baulé nation.

Tadjo, Véronique. *La Légende d'Abla Poku, Reine des Baulé.* L'Arbre à Palabres (N° 18 Janvier, 2006). http://www.revues-plurielles.org/_uploads/pdf/13_18_6.pdf.

p. 70   Other examples of a call to arms include the War of Asikaso between Anyii Dwabene and French colonial forces, in which Yaw Fum, king of Dwabene, was clear aggressor.

Sié, Koffi (1976). *Les Agni-Diabè, Histoire et Societé*, p. 138, 173. Université de Paris I Pantheon–Sorbonne.

p. 70   And in the nineteenth century, the Baulé mounted a couple Wars of Liberation against French colonialists.

Webster, J.B. and Boahen, Adu (1967). *The Growth of African Civilization: The Revolutionary*

Years - West Africa Since 1800, pp. 249–251. Longmans.

Chapter 9—Identity and Heritage

p. 72   As if to echo the above sentiment, in recent years, a few individuals have launched an all-Anyii cultural festival. Le Festival des Arts et de la Culture Agni (Festival of Anyii Arts and Culture) brings together all ten Agni subgroups to celebrate a common heritage and to cement linguistic and historical ties.

FESTACI: http://www.festaci.org.

p. 71   The Chokosi, a community located in the north of Togo.

Twi.bb (online dictionary for the Twi language of the Akan people of Ghana in West Africa): *Chokosi.*   http://www.twi.bb/akan-people-chokosi.php.

p. 73   ... the ECOWAS protocol on the free movement of persons and goods.

http://www.comm.ecowas.int/departments/trade-custom-free-movement/.

p. 74   Until independence in 1957 and the mass education policy of Kwame Nkrumah, Ghana's first president.

Bonney, Emmanuel. *Nkrumah's Educational Legacy:*

http://www.modernghana.com/news/239452/1/
nkrumah039s-educational-legacy.html.

p. 75   ... the decision to build a school at Nkrankwanta was not out of character of the Anyii, because by 1920, when most traditional rulers elsewhere had no formal education, Anyii Dwabene had crowned the educated Ndaa Kwasi king.

Sié, Koffi (1976). *Les Agni-Diabè, Histoire et Societé*, pp. 57, 61, 182. Université de Paris I Pantheon–Sorbonne.

Chapter 11—A Window into Anyii Culture and Society

p. 92   Though Yaa Asantewaa was defeated and later taken prisoner and exiled to the Indian Ocean island of Seychelles along with King Agyemang Prempeh I, where she died, she had shown strong-willed decision making and bravery on the battlefield as most male compatriots shook in cowardice.

Wikipedia: https://en.wikipedia.org/wiki/Yaa_Asantewaa.

What Nana Yaa Asantewaa, queen mother of Ejisu, said:

"Now I have seen that some of you fear to go forward to fight for our king. If it were in the brave days of, the days of Osei Tutu, Okomfo Anokye, and Opoku Ware, chiefs would not sit down to see their king taken away without firing a shot. No white man could have dared to speak to chief

of the Ashanti in the way the Governor spoke to you chiefs this morning. Is it true that the bravery of the Ashanti is no more? I cannot believe it. It cannot be! I must say this: if you the men of Ashanti will not go forward, then we will. We the women will. I shall call upon my fellow women. We will fight the white men. We will fight till the last of us falls in the battlefields."
http://www.ghanaweb.com/GhanaHomePage/people/person.php?ID=175.

p. 92   In nation building and political leadership, there are a few examples where female leaders led their people to found new kingdoms or ruled existing ones. For example, Nana Afia Dokua ruled Akyem Abuakwa from 1817 to 1835.
"The story of Okyeman cannot be told without mentioning Nana Dokua who at one time was both Okyehene (King) and Ohemaa (Queenmother) and led the Akyem forces on the battle field of Akatamanso in 1826."
History of Akyem Abuakwa, http://pallionghana. com/projects/etwienana/cms/okyeman/history-of-akyem-abuakwa.

p. 92   Abena Pokua led her people from Mampong Nsuta in present-day Ghana to migrate and found the kingdom of Baulé in present-day Cote d'Ivoire.
Ghana Rising, http://ghanarising.blogspot.ca/2013/01/ghanas-history-ghanaian-women-in-power.html.

p. 92 Nana Dwaben Serwaa led her people from Asante Dwaben to establish the new kingdom of New Dwaben in present-day south-central Ghana, where she ruled wisely and effectively.

"… concurrent Queen and King of Dwaben. First enstooled as the Queen of Dwaben and held the joint offices until 1963, when she placed her son, Nana Kwabena Boateng II on the male Stool of Dwaben, making him Dwabenhene. She continued to rule as Dwabenhemaa until 1969, when she abdicated."

Ghana Rising, http://ghanarising.blogspot.ca/search?q=dwaben+serwaa.

p. 103 The belief system recognizes what some writers have called "the living dead," where the dead live in an outer world but within a comfortable reach of mortals.

Mbiti, John S. (1990). *African Religions & Philosophy*, pp. 74–87. Heinemann.

p. 104 The interesting thing is that quite often the person whose life is being celebrated at a great cost did not receive much attention or love from the very extended family that is mourning his or her death. The late K. Gyasi, a famous Ghanaian highlife musician of all time, masterfully captured the contradiction in one of his songs:

"ɔmama sɛ mere bɛ wu a, me nnim" … (I know not when a noble heart like me is going to die)

https://www.youtube.com/watch?v=Ynz1vYeFx_g.

Chapter 13—The Anyii at Play

p. 126 Perhaps it is because the popular highlife music that is almost synonymous with Ghana evolved in English-speaking West Africa to the exclusion of the French colonies …
Encyclopedia Britannica. *High-Life: African Music.*
http://www.britannica.com/art/High-Life-African-music.
Ghanaweb. *The Origins of High Life in Ghana.*
http://www.ghanaweb.com/GhanaHomePage/audio/
The-Origins-of-High-Life-in-Ghana-191061.

p. 127 From the first recognized highlife recording in Ghana in 1928, which was a love song extoling the beauty of Yaa Amponsah, and of the same title, the immediate pre- and postindependence era produced some of the greatest traditional highlife music artistes in Ghana and West Africa. Kumase Trio, led by Kwame Asare, singing "Yaa Amponsah" in 1928: https://www.youtube.com/watch?v=abElmhTW_Zw.

p. 127 "Kofi Nkrabea" and "Yaw Berko," a couple of the group's most successful songs, touched the sensibilities of almost every young Anyii-Baulé lover of highlife music. The narratives in both "Kofi Nkrabea" and "Yaw Berko" are the travails of a young man of the same names whose very names "Nkrabea" and "Berko," which translate as "Destiny" and "Born to Struggle," respectively, had spelled bad luck since the day each person was born. It was obvious the song resonated well with many young Anyii-Baulé men fighting uphill battles in life.

The African Brothers Band singing "Kofi Nkrabea": https://www.youtube.com/watch?v=AE6qI5IfHWg.

p. 127   … Akan Anyii-Baulé has not been devoid of talent in popular music. Trailblazers in dance music have been, among others, Les Soeurs Comoe (the Comoe Sisters), a sister-sister duo whose renditions not only touched on the issues of the day but also on the rights of women. In their "Adja me dede …" release in the early 1960s, Les Soeurs Comoe at once exposed and lamented the inhumanity and cruelty among some men who would toil and suffer in poverty with a woman, only to divorce her, with no property rights, to marry a younger woman who would reap where she had not sowed. But the group hit the top of the charts with their "Abidjan pon so" release, which commemorated the completion of the grand project of a major bridge across the Ebrie Lagoon in Abidjan.

Les Soeurs Comoe singing "Abidjan pon so": https://www.youtube.com/watch?v=d0XEuPr6Mvg.

p. 128 In Antoinette Konan, the audience is treated to a powerful rendition of traditional Baulé songs, arranged in the best of modern acoustics and percussions, and delivered in a voice as rich and controlled as the culture it showcases.

Antoinette Konan in flight, doing "Abidjan Dja": https://www.youtube.com/watch?v=penK2mR79D4.

KORA Awards: http://koraawards.com/.

F. Kenya singing "Awiélеε" ("Awieε" in Twi). "Awiélеε, biala nze" (None knows how he will end up in life): https://www.youtube.com/watch?v=XMXZtpKlODI.

In "Vis-à-Vis," Frederic Desire Ehui and his Meiway band give a dancehall touch to a popular traditional Nzema song: https://www.youtube.com/watch?v=6TDn8xPK_5c.

Appendix

p. 145 "Much of the collective Akan civilization is originated from Begho, a town located immediately south of the Black Volta."

Begho (also *Bighu* or *Bitu*; called *Bew* and *Nsokↄ/ Nsawkaw* by the Akan) was an ancient trading town located just south of the Black Volta at the transitional zone between the forest and savanna (present-day Ghana, northwestern Brong-Ahafo Region). The town, like Bono-Manso, was of considerable importance as an entrepot frequented by northern caravans from Mali from around AD 1100. Goods traded included ivory, salt, leather, gold, kola nuts, cloth, and copper alloys.

Excavations have laid bare walled structures dated between AD 1350 and 1750, as well as pottery of all kinds, smoking pipes, and evidence of iron smelting. With a probable population of more than ten thousand, Begho was one of the largest towns in the southern part of <u>West Africa</u> at the time of the arrival of the <u>Portuguese</u> in 1471.

Wikipedia: https://en.wikipedia.org/wiki/Bonoman.

p. 145 Later, Bonomanso, also located south of the Black Volta but closer to present-day Takyiman, succeeded Begho in the formation of collective Akan culture and civilization.

Davidson, Basil, Buah, F.K., and Ajayi, J.F. Ade (1966). *A History of West Africa.* (New York: Doubleday), pp. 76–77.

HISTORY

Around the end of the seventeenth century, the Anyii Dwabene—an Akan tribe originally located in the Amansie area of present-day Ghana—leave their homeland to found a new kingdom at Dadieso, also in Ghana. But the Anyii Dwabene become liberators when they intervene in a war to save the kingdom of Abron Bondoukou. Eventually, they establish a new home and a new kingdom with capital at AnyiniBileKro, in what is now Cote d'Ivoire. Later, a section of Anyii Dwabene resists French colonialism and leaves to found a settlement across the border in the then Gold Coast, calling it Nkrankwanta. The story of Nkrankwanta is a story of freedom and liberty.

In *Cultural Migration—A Short History of Nkrankwanta and Anyii Dwabene*, author Zac Adama is privileged to share the oral history of Nkrankwanta in the print form for the first time. Exploring the lives of the first immigrants of Nkrankwanta—men and women who chose danger and uncertainty over servitude and complacency—it is the story of a people who explored the unknown for new possibilities and opportunities, and who wanted their story to be told to generations after them. Not only a book of history, *Cultural Migration—A Short History of Nkrankwanta and Anyii Dwabene* explores a comparative linguistic study between Akan Twi-Fante, spoken mainly in Ghana, and Akan Anyii-Baule, whose majority speakers live in neighbouring Côte d'Ivoire.

The story of Nkrankwanta is essentially a story of migration. It is partly the story of a people who liberated others and, in turn, required assistance when they were faced with imminent danger. The story of Nkrankwanta speaks to the human heart—it portrays the changing fortunes in the lives of a people who have, with each step along the way, been purposeful and determined.

ZAC ADAMA is a native son of Nkrankwanta and has extensive instruction in Akan history. He has a mastery of both the Twi and Anyii languages, the latter being his mother tongue. He is currently an information technology professional who lives and works in Calgary, Canada, and he has a background in philosophy that drives his unquenchable curiosity about the nature of things.

iUniverse®
www.iuniverse.com

Printed in the United States
By Bookmasters